Thoughts on the Pot

Thoughts on the Pot

A Kaleidoscopic Cornucopia
of Jokes, Observations, and Advice

Pat Duke

ARCHWAY
PUBLISHING

Archway Publishing books may be ordered through booksellers or by contacting:

Archway Publishing
1663 Liberty Drive
Bloomington, IN 47403
www.archwaypublishing.com
844-669-3957

ISBN: 978-1-6657-2580-4 (sc)
ISBN: 978-1-6657-2578-1 (hc)
ISBN: 978-1-6657-2579-8 (e)

Library of Congress Control Number: 2022911591

Print information available on the last page.

Archway Publishing rev. date: 11/17/2022

I have consistently dedicated all the awards I've received in show business to my brother, John Duke, because he supported my career and gave me encouragement in every way possible.

For *Thoughts on The Pot*, there was one person, every day, who listened to every joke, advised me, and supported my efforts to finish this silliness. That lovely person was my wonderful wife, Sally Hewlett—the love of my life!

sally Hewlett, 1/8/1953 to 10/15/2019

"Laughter and tears are both responses to frustration and exhaustion. I myself prefer to laugh, since there is less cleaning up to do afterward."

–KURT VONNEGUT

warning

These are jokes. They are intended for entertainment purposes only. None of these jokes are about you, even if I used your name. If I used your name, it was meant as an homage to you. You must be very special to have a joke written about you. I bow before your greatness, sir or madam.

Introduction

Friends tell me jokes all the time, but I've had a hard time remembering them. So several years ago, I decided to start collecting them like a philatelist. (I know, sounds dirty. It's stamp collecting, ya perv.)

Musicians and actors tell me the best jokes. And since most of my friends are musicians and actors, there isn't a day that goes by without one of them saying, "Hey Pat, did ya hear the one about the … (insert dirty joke here)?"

Am I in any way embarrassed to put out a book of dirty jokes? Heck no. This vast collection of dirty jokes places this book in good company. Wolfgang Amadeus Mozart kept a notepad with him at all times. On it, he amassed a great number of fart, piss, poop, and sex jokes, which he cherished sharing with his friends. William Shakespeare, perhaps the greatest writer the English language has ever known, loved writing dirty jokes in his plays. Not just a little, *a lot*. He chose to insert his bawdy jokes in the most incredibly inappropriate places. Gentlemen, I salute you.

Collecting all these bawdy, blue, dirty jokes (well, some are actually clean) took a lot of years and came from a lot of sources, which explains why this book is all over the map, all over the road, careening out of control, crashing, burning—oh, the humanity—but I digress.

Mostly, these itty-bitty ditties are for "men of a certain age" about work, retirement, marriage, divorce, drinking, drugs, religion, obesity, vegans, kids, parents, life, death, sleep, farts, and poop—all the stuff we're not supposed to talk about, but we do. They're mostly jokes, but occasionally, there will be a glimpse into my life as a voice actor, along with some quasi-sage advice here and there, served straight up with a twist or flat-out weird.

Covering all the bases, there are a total of three "groaners" in here, six Golden Oldies, and a tendency to channel Rodney Dangerfield. I don't know where that comes from. Is it politically correct? No. Is it misogynistic? No. (Well, maybe a little.) Honestly, I love women. And women? Why are you reading this? Stop. *Thoughts on the Pot* might piss you right off (and give me another joke to write). One more thing: *no political jokes*. Late-night comedians aptly cover those.

So, pull up a throne and sit for a while. There are almost a thousand or so farcically, foolish funnies coming your way. The first section is for short jokes; let's call it "Quick Hits." The second section is for the longer story jokes; let's call that section "Long Tokes." Take your time digesting them—and don't forget to flush.

One more thing: if you're easily offended, you will be here. I am an equal-opportunity offender. Relax; most of the jokes are on me. Now, if you can't laugh at yourself, feel free to point and laugh at somebody else. This is the biggest collection of jokes ever collected. Take your time, enjoy the ride, and laugh your butt off.

Here we go!

QUiCK HitS

My doctor advised me to start killing people. Not in those exact words, of course; he just said that I have to lower the amount of stress in my life.

How does an attorney sleep? First, he lies on one side; then he lies on the other.

A man walks up to a hot woman sitting alone at the bar. He says, "Hi, beautiful. I'm a politician and an honest man." She says, "Hi, sugar. I'm a prostitute and a virgin."

You know who I hate? I hate guys who use big words just to make themselves look perspicacious.

Have you ever wanted to lie completely naked on a bearskin rug in front of a roaring fireplace? Me too, but I discovered that it's frowned upon at Cracker Barrel.

When we go camping, why do we have to use leaves as toilet paper, when bears are using Charmin?

My grandfather has the heart of a lion and a lifetime ban from the San Diego Zoo.

My grandmother said to me, "Chivalry is dead. What happened to you men? You don't even open doors anymore!" Defensively, I replied, "Yes, we do, Grandma. How do you think I got in here?"

It always surprises me when I meet someone for the very first time and know immediately that I want to spend the rest of my life without them.

What did the Grateful Dead fan say when he ran out of weed? "Man, this music sucks!"

I failed my driver's test today. The instructor asked me, "What do you do at a red light?" I said, "I usually call my wife, check my email, and see what people are up to on Facebook."

I asked my loving wife, Sally, if I was the only one she'd been with. She said, "Yes, Pat; all the others were nines and tens."

If women ruled the world, there would be no more wars, but there would be a bunch of jealous countries refusing to speak to each other.

A day at the dog beach gets kinda lonely when your dog's name is Shark.

———

My best friend got so drunk last night at the country club that when he staggered to the bar to get another drink, he won the dance contest.

———

Some people manage stress with exercise, yoga, and meditation. Others manage stress with prayer and long walks. I manage stress with sarcasm, cursing, and bourbon.

———

I used to have a goldfish that could break dance on carpet, but only for twenty seconds, and only once.

———

Surround yourself with people who have issues—because people who have issues always have alcohol.

———

It's been over a year since I joined my gym and not one damn thing has changed. I have a good mind to go down there to see what's going on.

———

Annoyed, the cashier said, "Strip down, facing me." How was I to know she meant my debit card?

———

It's a sad commentary on modern society that an entire loving family can be torn apart by such a simple thing as a pack of wild dogs.

Like most guys, I may have occasionally fantasized about going to bed with two beautiful women. In reality, that would be great for the women involved. This way, when I fall asleep, they'll at least have someone to talk to.

My grief counselor died yesterday. Thankfully, he was so good, I didn't give a shit.

I bet you didn't know that people write "congrats" because they don't know how to spell "congratchulayshuns."

I live on a street with a family of Jehovah's Witnesses. And no matter how many times I tell them no, they still come to my door every day and ask me to stop throwing rocks at their house.

A man gets the words *I love you* tattooed on his penis. He goes home to his wife and she says, "Stop trying to put words in my mouth."

A man goes into his son's room. He says to his son, "Son, if you keep masturbating, you're going to go blind." The boy says, "I'm over here, Dad."

A bear and a rabbit were taking a dump in the woods. The bear asked the rabbit, "Do you have a problem with poop sticking to your fur?" And the rabbit answered, "No, I don't." So, the bear wiped his butt with the rabbit.

The inventor of autocorrect died yesterday. His funnel is tomato.

How do I define marriage? Simple. Marriage is two people constantly asking each other what they want to eat until one of them dies.

A priest, a rabbit, and a minister walk into a bar. The bartender asks the rabbit, "What'll ya have?" The rabbit says, "I dunno; I'm only here because of autocorrect."

I've gotten pretty good at ventriloquism. Today, I totally freaked out my proctologist.

Last night, I was making love to my girlfriend and I said, "You have a tight puss and no tits." So she yelled, "Get off my back!"

What do you get when you cross a genius with a hooker? A fucking know-it-all.

When I was a young man, a girl I was dating said to me, "Hit me hard with all eight inches!" So I banged her twice with four inches and punched her in the nose.

Lately, I've been getting lovesick. That's what I call it. My doctor calls it chlamydia.

Women fall in love with what they hear. Men fall in love with what they see. That's why women wear makeup and men lie.

The real reason the Ten Commandments can't be displayed in a courthouse is because "Thou shalt not steal," "Thou shalt not commit adultery," and "Thou shalt not lie" have no place in a building full of lawyers.

Upon seeing a fishing lure in the water, the minnow asked, "Mama, what's that?" The mama fish replied, "It's that damn slut your father ran off with last year!"

I wish I were ten feet tall. I wouldn't have to jump to dunk a basketball. And I'd finally be the right height for my weight.

My wife wrecked the car again last night. She's fine, just a little shaken up. She told the policeman that the guy she ran into was talking on his phone and drinking a beer. The cop told her the man can do whatever he wants in his own living room.

What do you get when you mix LSD with birth control? A trip without the kids.

I know this guy who went on a serious health kick. He joined a gym, got a personal trainer, gave up drinking, and became a vegetarian. He was the picture of health right up to the moment he killed himself.

Over cocktails, my dad asked me why I drink so much. I said, "I drink to forget." He asked, "To forget what?" I said, "I don't remember."

When I'm quiet, my wife always wants to know what I'm thinking. I'm thinking nothing. I've got nothing. My brain has flatlined. My response? "Just sitting here thinking about how lucky I am to have you in my life." Works every time.

A man in an insane asylum yells, "I am Napoleon!" The doctor asks him how he knows this, and he says, "God told me." Just then, an inmate from another room yells, "I did *not*!"

I go to bed early and never miss an opportunity for a nap. Why? Because I promised my mom I would never give up on my dreams.

If last night's Mexican fiesta has you emitting methane toxicity, here's what you do. When you feel a big blast coming on, gather your family around and ask, "Is someone baking cookies?" They'll all take a big whiff.

For us, it's morning coffee and reading our email. For dogs, it's a morning walk and reading their pee mail.

Uncomfortable with evolution, some like to explain our existence using the term "intelligent design." But when you look at the female anatomy, what's so intelligent about putting a playground in a sewer?

I believe terrorists and mass murderers are always men because women prefer to kill their prey slowly, over many years.

Light travels faster than sound. That's why some people appear bright until you hear them speak.

My wife and I were flying back from our Cancun honeymoon. The flight attendant was getting our cocktails and making light conversation. She asked, "How did you find the weather on your honeymoon?" I said, "I stepped outside, and there it was."

FYI for women who are consistently attracted to alpha males: shy guys don't cheat on their wives.

I believe the reason Santa is so jolly is because he knows where all the naughty girls live.

Having dogs is good for your health. You walk, throw a ball, bend over to pick up poop. And your protein intake increases dramatically thanks to all the meals that now include dog hair.

Did you know that by replacing your morning coffee with green tea, you can reduce by 87 percent what little joy you have left in your life?

"What time is it?"
"Hell if I know. Pass me my trombone and I'll find out."
I give a few loud blasts on the trombone.
Someone shouts, "Who's that playing a damned trombone at two in the morning?"

When someone says, "It's nice to meet you," I think to myself, *Give it time.*

After a big fight, I shouted at my ex, "I was a fool when I married you!" She shouted back, "I know, but I was in love and didn't notice!"

Today, the temperature suddenly dropped from 90 to 55. I guess the weather saw a state trooper.

A little old lady on the bus hands the bus driver some peanuts. He thanks her and munches down. Every few minutes, she hands him more. Finally, the bus driver asks why she doesn't eat the peanuts. She says, "Look, I don't have any teeth; I just like to suck the chocolate off 'em."

In vino veritas is the exact reason why you can never trust a man who doesn't drink.

A tree house is the biggest insult to a tree. It's like saying, "I just killed a bunch of your friends, and now I want you to hold them."

A buddy of mine went to the doctor's office.
Doctor asked, "What brings you in today?"
He whispered, "Umm, Doc, I … ugh ... I have five penises."
Puzzled, the doctor asked, "How do your pants fit?"
Buddy replied, "Like a glove."

When someone begins a sentence with *truthfully* or *honestly,* I can assure you they are lying. And if they say, "Believe me," *don't.*

What happens when you give Viagra to a lawyer? He gets taller.

Years ago, I was driving with my three kids in the backseat. Two of them were screaming at each other, and the little one was crying her eyes out. That's when I saw a sign that said, "Watch for children," and I thought, *Wow, that's a pretty good deal.*

What does the sign on an out-of-business brothel say? "We're closed. Beat it."

The word *stress* is an anagram. It stands for: *s*hit *t*o *r*emember *e*very *s*ingle *s*econd.

The truth will set you free from having to remember all the lies you told that got you where you are today.

How is having sex like playing bridge? If you've got a great hand, you don't need a partner.

Sometimes I think I'd like to turn back the hands of time. With everything I know now, I would be the king of my high school. Then I remember algebra.

———————

Jimmy: "I love your new wife. She's so sweet and intelligent. The complete opposite of your first wife."
Me: "Really, how so?"
Jimmy: "Well, if you don't mind me saying, your ex was obnoxious, rude, loud, and stupid. Good riddance, buddy! How'd you get rid of her?"
Me: "It was easy."
Jimmy: "Really?"
Me: "Yeah. She said my friends were too damn judgmental, so she dumped me."

———————

People who live in glass houses shouldn't throw stones naked.

———————

I saw this guy at the gym wearing a sweatshirt that said, "Your Workout Is My Warm-up." And I thought, *I need a sweatshirt that says, "My Casual Drinking Is Your Alcohol Poisoning."*

———————

I believe if you eat and drink like no one will ever see you naked, you will be right.

———————

I am so sick of all the negative Irish stereotypes. As soon as I finish this Guinness, I'm going to punch somebody out.

My teenage daughter got mad at me and screamed, "I hate you! I don't want to be your daughter anymore; *I quit!*" So I said, "What, no two-week notice? I hope you're not expecting a good reference."

Pharmaceutical companies have come up with a remarkable new diet pill. It's called LSD. Turns out, it's impossible to raid the fridge when it's being guarded by fire-breathing dragons.

A chimpanzee moves quickly through the jungle, grabbing one vine and letting go of another. If he doesn't let go of the vine behind him, his progress stops. Like him, we can't move forward while hanging onto the past.

How do you know a Korean thief broke into your house? Your math homework is done and your dog is missing.

It's illegal to drink and drive, so why do I need a driver's license to buy beer?

I was walking home last night and decided to take a shortcut through the cemetery. Three girls came running up to me and explained that they were frightened to walk in the cemetery at night, so I agreed to let them walk with me. I told them, "I completely understand. I used to be scared to walk through the cemetery at night, too—when I was alive."

When I was a kid, I could go to the store with a buck and come home with three bags of chips, two Snickers, Pixie Sticks, bubble gum and a Coke. Now they have cameras everywhere.

If you take away his looks, money, intelligence, talent, charm, and success, there's really no difference between me and George Clooney.

I had dinner at my friend Kim's house. She has three cats. All night, she talked to them like they could understand what she was saying. When I got home, I told my dog, Chelsea, all about it, and we laughed and laughed.

Am I the only one who counts getting up out of a chair as a sit-up? Having dogs helps—forty-eight, forty-nine, fifty!

There are two secrets to enjoying an excellent bottle of wine. First, remove the cork to allow the wine to breathe. Second, if it looks like it's not breathing, give it mouth to mouth.

I was in a band in high school. We weren't very good. We didn't know any party songs; we just got up on stage and jammed, but we were cheap. We mainly played at forced retirement parties and shotgun weddings.

My dad told me he was considering getting one of those walk-in tubs. The problem is, you have to sit there while it fills up and while it drains, and they cost $5,000. I told him he should get one of those computerized Japanese bidets. They can cost five grand too, but they come pre-loaded with magic and miracles.

I patted his head and said, "Good boy! Does he bite?" For some reason, that really pissed off a random Walmart shopper with her son on a leash.

I believe it is time to stop asking vegans if they miss meat. Vegans don't miss meat. They miss their friends. They miss their families. But not meat.

I keep Tums in my pocket for no reason at all. I used to carry condoms, but today, I've got a much better chance of getting heartburn than getting laid.

Long ago, I had a real job, nine to five, with a desk and everything. I hated it. I decided to quit. I told my wife. She took it about as well as could be expected. I didn't tell my dog. I didn't want her to worry. I was afraid she would try to run away to find her real parents.

I live in Nashville, Tennessee. I love it. There's a church on almost every corner. They say forgiveness is divine. It must be because the other corners seem to be reserved exclusively for strip clubs.

Everyone knows the five-second rule for food dropped on the floor, but that doesn't work if you have a two-second dog.

First woman in space to Mission Control: "Houston, we have a problem."
Mission Control: "What is it?"
First woman: "Never mind."
Mission Control: "What seems to be the problem?"
First woman: "Nothing."

Mission Control: "Please tell us; we really need to know."
First woman: "Just go on about your business. Forget I'm even here."
Mission Control: "We can't do that. Now please tell us what's wrong!"
First woman: "Well, if you don't know, far be it from me to tell you what to do."

Do you know where virgin wool comes from? Ugly sheep.

I was walking down Michigan Avenue in Chicago when I was astonished to see a beautiful homeless woman. She smiled, so I asked if I could take her home. She blushed and excitedly said, "Sure." But her expression quickly changed when I walked away with her cardboard box.

Job interview:
Boss: "That's a firm handshake for a girl."
Sally: "That's a small bulge for a man."
Boss: "Your mother loved it."
Sally: "My mother died."
Boss: "Of exhaustion."
Sally: "From laughing at you."
Boss: "See you Monday morning at nine a.m."

For the single guys among us, there are two important rules to follow until your wedding day: one, never chase when you can replace; and two, never buy when you can rent.

My wife got me an appointment with a new internist, Dr. B. Gee. Apparently, all his patients are "Stayin' Alive." (*Groan*)

Have you ever noticed how some women ignore the nice guys, chase the jerks, then spend the rest of their lives complaining about them?

Every year, I've made the same stupid New Year's resolution: "I'm going to quit drinking." Not this year, because I have finally come to the conclusion that nobody likes a quitter.

Alcohol does not have all the answers, but it does help you forget all the annoying questions.

I enjoy a nice glass of wine every night for its health benefits. The other glasses are for my witty comebacks and flawless dance moves.

What do you call a woman who is paralyzed from the waist down? Married.

There's a brand of cigarettes made by Native Americans called American Spirit. They must be healthy for us. I can't imagine any reason why Native Americans would want to harm us.

As a lover of life and an eternal optimist, I like to say, "Don't worry so much. Someday, someone is going to love you and hug you so tight that all the sharp broken pieces inside you will get pressed into your internal organs, killing you and ending your suffering."

We have a border-collie mix. He was "fixed" two years ago. He's still trying to hump our female goldendoodle every chance he gets. He has no balls! It's embarrassing. Here's how bad it is: we can't take him anywhere. If anyone tries to pet him, *boi-oi-oing*, pink lipstick.

My wife sent me a text on a cold January morning: "Windows frozen, won't open!"
I responded to her text: "Carefully pour lukewarm water over it, and then gently tap the edges with a hammer."

Ten minutes later, my wife sent me this text: "Computer really screwed up now!"

Men are more afraid of snakes than women. But women are a close second.

It should be common knowledge by now that a good deed will always come back to bite you in the ass.

The waitress comes by for our drink orders and says, "Okay, guys, what's your poison?"
Budweiser salesman: "I'll have a Bud Light."
Miller salesman: "Miller Lite for me."
Coors salesman: "I'll have a Coors Light."
Guinness salesman: "Make mine an iced tea."
Everyone stares at him in disbelief.
Guinness salesman replies: "What? If you guys aren't going to drink beer, neither am I!"

Women, are you sick of jerks hitting on you? And they won't stop, even when you tell them you have a man? You want them to stop? Don't tell them you *have* a man; tell them you used to *be* a man.

Every Christmas, we have pigs in blankets. Or, as you might say, my in-laws in the guest bedroom.

FYI, you should pee on a jellyfish sting, not a jelly stain. Again, apologies to the lady at the Waffle House this morning.

I was out with friends at a local dive bar. As we were leaving, a policeman said to me, "Do you realize that you are staggering?" So I said, "Why, thank you; you're pretty handsome yourself." We laughed and laughed and laughed. And now I need one of you to pay my bail.

I think when people play Christmas music in September, it should be legal for me to kill them and use their bodies as Halloween decorations.

I once told my wife that when I die, I hope it's while we're making love. She quipped, "I hope you're right; that way, we know it'll be quick."

I checked into a hotel, and on the side table next to the bed was a Bible. I opened that Bible, and on the first page was written: "If you are an alcoholic, if you have a drinking problem, call this number." So I picked up the phone and called that number—it was a liquor store.

She told me that she missed me. Normally, that would be comforting, but I could see that she was reloading.

When I take a walk in the forest, I marvel at how many lovers have carved their initials in trees. I stop and stare at them and I wonder, *How many guys feel the need to bring a knife on a date?*

The best feeling in the world is sleeping next to the one you love, all the while knowing they have no idea how you managed to get into their house.

This morning as I was buttoning my shirt, a button fell off. After that, I picked up my briefcase and the handle fell off. Then I went to open the door, and the doorknob fell off. I went to get into my car, and the door handle came off in my hand. And now? Well, now I'm afraid to pee.

When you give yourself completely to someone, you give them the power to destroy you. It's still worth it.

"You're the bomb!" "No, you're the bomb!" In the United States, that's a compliment. In the Middle East, that's an argument.

———

Here's one I need to clear up. It turns out that marijuana actually is a gateway drug—to the fridge.

———

Once, I was driving to a recording studio in Burbank, California. On the way, I saw a girl with pink hair, another girl with electric-blue hair, a tiny girl walking a Great Dane as big as a horse, and a shirtless guy tatted from head to toe walking a pot-bellied pig. I love LA.

———

"Thank you for your continued patience. Please remain on the line and one of our knowledgeable representatives will be with you shortly. In the meantime, please enjoy our complimentary Muzak, fully distorted for your dining and dancing pleasure."

———

The phone rings; the wife answers. The perv on the line is breathing heavily and whispers, "I bet you have a tight ass with no hair." She calmly replies, "I sure do. He's right here watching golf. Who shall I say is calling?"

———

My girlfriend said there's no spark between us anymore. So I tased her.

Laughter is the best medicine. It really is. They've done scientific studies that prove that people who laugh a lot actually do live longer than people with terminal cancer.

Diets and religions have a lot in common. They both do everything they can to limit our participation in the activities we love.

I am attracted to women with hoarse, raspy voices. I figure maybe they're all done screaming.

Do you know what you get when you mix beans and onions? Tear gas. (*Groan*)

What's the difference between a catfish and a lawyer? One's a slimy, scum-sucking, bottom-feeding scavenger; the other is a fish.

Why was the lawyer skimming the Bible right before he died? He was looking for loopholes.

My only blonde joke:
A blonde calls American Airlines. She asks, "How long are your flights from America to England?"
The woman on the other end of the phone says, "Just a minute."
The blonde says, "Thanks!" and hangs up the phone.

John's boss called him into his office and told him that if he married his daughter, he could have a $100,000 raise and a brand-new Mercedes-Benz. John replied, "So what's wrong with her?"

It's not new, and I don't know who said this first, but it's too perfect not to include. Surprise sex first thing in the morning is a great way to start your day—unless you're in prison.

Once, I told my ex that as a man, I am a lot like a fine wine, getting better with age. The next day, she locked me in the wine cellar.

I went gator hunting in Louisiana with the "King of the Swamp," Troy Landry. The first time I saw a twelve-foot alligator up close, my sphincter could have cracked walnuts.

My son was really into astronomy. One evening, when he was about ten years old, we were outside studying the night sky with a telescope when he asked, "Daddy, how do stars die?" I replied, "Well, son, as bright as they shine, they usually die from a drug overdose."

Dogs sleep twenty hours a day. The rest of the time, they eat, lick, scratch, poop, pee, and love.

I'm going to create a new Facebook account, and the name will be Nobody. That way, when I see stupid crap people post, I can "like" it and it will say, "Nobody likes this."

I don't have statistics or a pie chart to back this up. But it seems to me that the more money spent on a wedding, the more likely it is to end in divorce.

The difference between drunk and stoned explained: if you're out and you see five drunk guys, there's probably gonna be a fight. If you're out and you see five stoned guys, they're probably gonna start a band.

FYI: Eternal love is a myth. The concepts of a soul mate or some kind of marital destiny are not only a fantasy; they're mathematically impossible.

If my backyard were emo, would it cut itself?

I believe I drink responsibly. I don't drive, I'm usually at home, and I seldom spill.

A little girl cuts her hand on the playground and runs, crying, to the teacher. She asks the teacher for a glass of cider for her hand.

"Why do you want a glass of cider?" the teacher asks.
"To take away the pain," sobs the little girl.
"What do you mean?" the teacher asks.
"Well," sobs the little girl, "I overheard my big sister say that whenever she has a prick in her hand, she can't wait to get it in cider."

A man goes to a twenty-dollar hooker and contracts crabs. When he goes back to complain, the hooker laughs and says, "What did you expect for twenty bucks, lobster?"

I once dated a girl who was a twin. My buddies were curious; how could I tell them apart? Well, Jill paints her fingernails purple, and Jack has a penis.

This is a great assurance for your best friend. Just tell them that when their world comes crashing down around them, you promise to be right there beside them to say, "I told you so."

In Louisiana, everybody goes fishing. It's the law. And another thing: gas stations cook food. Yes, and it's really good. Last time I was down there, we had a nice sit-down lunch at a gas station. The sign out front cracked me up. It said, "Eat Here, Get Gas and Worms."

Dark shades let me see what I want and ignore the rest, a lot like Facebook.

"You are but dust, and to dust you will return." That's why I don't dust. It might be somebody I know.

My life is like a reality TV show on a life-sized screen with only one channel that I desperately need to change, but I can't find the remote.

A friend of mine posted a joke. In it, he used the word *retard*. I was livid.
I said, "Learning disabilities are not funny!"
He said, "They are if they're clever."
I replied, "With your logic, jokes about blind people are hilarious, as long as they're visual."

Around the house, I'm not exactly a man's man. I don't know crap about tools. I can't assemble or fix anything. But when my wife has a jar that needs opening, I am the Hulk.

Usually, men pay for everything. Mention that to your wife and you'll be paying for it till the end of time.

People say drug abuse is a horrible thing. I don't believe it. I'm an optimist; I look for the silver lining in all things. I say drug abuse is good. Without drugs, we would have a lot fewer home runs in baseball, and we wouldn't have any rock 'n' roll.

If at first you don't succeed, stay the hell away from skydiving.

This morning, my wife woke up with a big smile on her face. Man, I love Sharpies.

College football: bankrupting gamblers since 1908.

Some people I know are always overdressed, completely wrapped up in themselves.

My wife likes to fix things around the house. She's got a tool belt and everything. Right now, she's up on the roof replacing a floodlight, and she is two steps away from an insurance claim that will greatly improve my finances.

There's a huge difference between giving up and deciding you can't take this crap anymore.

Are you old enough to remember when dating was risk free? Young adulthood was a beautiful thing. Women were on the pill, and condoms were optional. No STDs, no AIDS, and then some party pooper went and ruined it for everyone by banging a monkey.

When you win awards, it feels great. Those trophies really are heavy. You make a little speech, people applaud, and you go home. You will eventually put them to good use as doorstops or paperweights.

I took French in high school and college. When I finally go to Paris, I will be perfectly qualified to ask a Frenchman for the location of the nearest bathroom.

Whenever someone tries to tell that light bulb joke, you know, how many blah-blah men does it take to screw in a lightbulb? The answer is always *one*. Why? Because given the chance, a man will pretty much screw anything.

When the person you see as the love of your life leaves you, you might believe they broke your heart. They didn't. The pain you feel proves your heart is working just fine. So, what did they break? Your trust. And that's forever.

TV is loaded with commercials for anti-aging creams. I'm not buying until they show a newborn baby covered in one of these magic creams who turns to the camera and says in a deep, manly voice, "Oops, I used too much."

A drunk driver is being arrested by a female police officer. She cuffs him, and just before she pushes him into the back seat of her squad car, she informs him, "Anything you say can and will be held against you." The drunk replies, "Boobies!"

So many medicines we take have restrictions when it comes to food. You either have to take them with a meal, or after a meal, or stand on your head and administer them anally. (Just kidding.) I take one daily that works even better on an empty stomach. You should give it a try. It helps you feel better in fifteen minutes or less. It's called "Martini."

What happens to you when you die? There's a new religion that claims your soul flies out of your body and gets stuck on the roof of your house. They're known as Frisbeetarians.

Lately, I've noticed people saying, "Let's hop on a conference call," or "I'll hop on the phone with you." That's a lot of hopping and something I'd really love to see.

A grasshopper walks into a bar, and the bartender says, "Hey, we have a drink named after you!" The grasshopper looks surprised and asks, "You have a drink named Steve?"

A friend of mine was a missionary in Iraq. It affected him deeply. At wit's end, he called the Suicide Hotline.
Hotline operator: "Hello, are you depressed?"
Friend: "Yes."
Operator: "Are you feeling suicidal?"
Friend: "Yes."
Operator: "Can you drive a truck?"

Billy Joe is in court for stealing a can of tomatoes. The judge says, "Billy Joe, seeing as how there are six tomatoes in that can, I'm gonna sentence you to six days in jail." All of a sudden, from the back of the courtroom, Billy Joe's ex-wife screams, "He stole a can of peas too!"

My cousin Dave called yesterday. He said he had a terrible sunburn and didn't know what to do.
I told Dave, "About an hour before you go to bed, take Viagra."
Frustrated, he asked, "How in the hell is that going to cure my sunburn?"
I said, "It won't, but it'll keep the sheets off of it."

Fighting a war for peace makes about as much sense as screwing for virginity.

I taught my dog Chelsea a lot of cool tricks. She's so smart, I actually taught her to roll over while she was asleep. She snores.

I believe you should know what you need, speak your mind, and keep the conversations focused. Because your therapist is infinitely more disturbed than you.

A priest was talking to a group of kids about "being good" and going to heaven. At the end of his talk, he asked, "Where do you want to go?"
"Heaven! Heaven!" yelled little Lisa.
"And what do you have to be to get there?" asked the priest.
"Dead! Dead!" yelled little Johnny.

Falling in love is all emotion and fantasy. The truth is, people change, and so does love. That's why divorce ... is good. It's not the end of a happy marriage; it's the start of a happy life. Sure, it's expensive, but so worth it.

In the checkout line at the grocery store, a complete stranger turned to me and started bragging. She said, "I have the perfect son. He doesn't smoke, he doesn't drink, and he doesn't hang out with loose women."
I said, "Congratulations, ma'am. How old is he?"
"My son's birthday is this Wednesday. He'll be six!"

For better or worse, in sickness and health, for richer, for poorer—within reason.

With the hope of solving all her problems, Alice in Wonderland keeps eating and drinking everything she sees—just like me.

My buddy Robert met a beautiful woman in a bar. He was charming, clever, and funny. He was winning. She gave him her number. He called it. Apparently, her boyfriend is a really nice guy.

Today, I shocked the hell out of our postman by opening the front door in the nude. I don't know what shocked him the most, my nudity or the fact that I knew where he lived.

I was okay driving home through the cemetery until the female voice on my GPS blurted out, "You have reached your final destination."

I was skeptical at first, but after examining the evidence, I have concluded that desserts make my clothes shrink.

I sat down for dinner at a restaurant, and the waiter asked, "Do you want to hear today's special?" I said, "Yes, please." The waiter said, "No problem, sir. Today is special."

I woke up this morning determined to drink less, eat right, and exercise. But that was four hours ago, when I was younger and full of hope.

I know the secret for making your spouse groan, *"Mmmm, mmmm, mmmm,"* all night long. It involves duct tape.

Arguing with a woman is like getting arrested. Everything you say can and will be used against you.

This one's for all the sadistic high school physical education teachers. Stop forcing fat kids to climb a rope. That's like expecting blind kids to excel at archery.

A woman walks into her dry cleaners' shop and says, "I've got another dress for you." The man behind the counter, who is a little hard of hearing, replies, "Come again?" The woman responds, "No, this time it's mustard."

Go to your room! Take a nap! You're grounded! You are not leaving this house! I recently came to the realization that my childhood punishments are now my adult dreams come true.

What's the deal with Twizzlers? They have the consistency of pencil erasers and taste like NyQuil-flavored birthday candles. So why can't I stop eating them?

Okay, guy-code stuff, here's the deal. If you know how to do the laundry, load the dishwasher, and make the bed, never ... *ever* ... let her know.

I often order food delivery from restaurants online. Regardless of the service, at the end of my order, they always ask if I will share the love on Facebook or Twitter. Share the love? I ordered food, not a Russian bride.

Celery. No fat, no sugar, no carbohydrates, and only six calories per stalk. The texture? Kinda crunchy. And the taste? Kinda bland. More people would eat celery if it came in flavors like Thin Mint.

It began with mapping the human genome. Now, through DNA research, science is on the verge of discovering how our children are born already knowing everything.

If smoking weed causes short-term memory loss, what does smoking weed do?

Whenever the brain and the heart fight, it's always the liver that suffers.

I'll do whatever it takes to lose weight and get in shape except dieting and exercising.

When looking for a proctologist, I suggest finding one with an Asian name. They're usually diminutive. The way I see it, if the doctor's finger is bigger than my penis, it's not an exam; it's a rape.

When I die, I hope I linger in a coma for a while so I can finally live the dream.

"Music will help you relax," said no musician ever.

My wife, Sally, watched Piglet's new comedy special on Netflix. She told me he would have been just as funny without all the Pooh jokes.

If you get kicked out of school for having sex, teaching is not for you.

Man or woman, I don't care who is piloting this plane unless it involves parallel parking.

Denigrating fat people accomplishes nothing. They have mirrors.

Because heavy traffic is a nightmare, if you want to get somewhere quickly in a big city, you need to make a lot of right turns. That's probably why I'll never understand NASCAR.

Every American teenage boy has an athletic sock he's fond of. It's glazed on the inside, like a Krispy Kreme doughnut.

Be prepared. If your house were to catch on fire tonight, are you sure you have enough marshmallows?

Yesterday, I went to Target to purchase a camouflaged shirt. They're really good. I couldn't find them anywhere.

Sixty-five percent of Americans are overweight, and 35 percent of those are morbidly obese, so what's up with the ever-decreasing size of the seats on commercial airplanes?

Exasperated husband: "Why don't you tell me when you're having an orgasm?" Wife: "You told me not to bother you at the office."

The FDA recently approved a new drug for men who are easily offended or can't take a joke. The new testicular-fortitude capsules will be available in most pharmacies soon under the brand names Growaset and Perkanut.

I called my dad on Father's Day. I discovered that he had added another TV. That makes *eight*. My next call was to the *Guinness Book of World Records*.

Golden Oldie: A friend of mine is a dyslexic agnostic insomniac. Every night, he lies awake wondering if there is a dog.

When people screw me over, I always forgive and forget, except when I'm holding a grudge.

You know that sound female tennis players make when they hit the ball? That's the sound I make getting up out of a chair.

A recent study proved that humans eat more bananas than monkeys. No surprise to me; I can't remember the last time I ate a monkey.

There are two essential rules to business management. First, the customer is always right. Second, they must be punished for their arrogance.

I love gummi bears. One day, when I inevitably choke to death on them, I hope people will just say that I was killed by bears and leave it at that.

Cannabis is a performance-enhancing drug if they're serving pizza at the finish line.

Do you want to make an elevator ride more fun? Change your ring tone to a fart noise.

I am in a same-sex marriage. It's just me, and it's always the same.

Gastroenterologist: the only guy I know who enjoys spending an entire day dealing with assholes.

Thanksgiving: the holiday that celebrates our yearly leap from satiated to self-loathing.

A lot of married guys tell me that when they watch TV, the remote never leaves their hands. They are in control. They are the masters of their domain, the kings of their castles. In my house, I watch what she wants or I watch alone.

I believe that making love with erectile dysfunction is like trying to shove a marshmallow in a coin slot.

My sinuses are messed up. I don't know if it's allergies, a sinus infection, or a bad case of boogie-woogie boogies.

I have to admit, when I was very young, I felt like a man trapped inside a woman's body. Then I was born.

At my age, my penis is like a semicolon. It's seldom used, and I can't remember what it's for.

Women marry to have kids and raise a family. Men get married because they don't want to die sick, miserable, and alone.

I was feeling good about myself, so I joined a gym. That's the best way I know to get rid of that pesky self-esteem.

For most of us, philanthropy is more than we can afford.

There are two things families should all be thankful for during the holidays: football and alcohol.

It's dreamy. It's free. It's fun. It's relaxing. It's rejuvenating. Is it porn? No, pervert; it's sleep.

Don't worry about me. I'm in a good place—not spiritually or emotionally. Okay, I'm in a bar.

It suddenly occurs to you that this will be your first and last date with a woman when she pronounces the *t* and *g* in *filet mignon.*

Violence, murders, and explosions. Video games have everything we American men love.

Dang, dern, dad-gummit, got-dern, heck, and gald-dang! If you're gonna live in the South, you have to learn how Southerners curse.

If you hate someone because of their race, creed, or religion, that is wrong. You need to get to know them first.

My kids treat me like God. They don't believe in me.

I'll tell you what. If I see one more person texting while they're driving, I'm gonna roll down my window and throw my beer at them.

Comfortably numb is so yesteryear. Today, there are strains of cannabis that are so powerful, they can turn a grown-ass man into a narcoleptic fainting goat—or so I've heard.

An Irish skeleton staggers into a pub on St. Patrick's Day and says, "Give me a pint of Guinness, a shot of Jameson, and a mop."

As I gazed at my naked body in the mirror, I thought, *Any minute now, I'm gonna get thrown out of Walmart.*

Mansplaining is always wrong, even when you know she's misinformed and delusional.

We often hear it said that we don't appreciate what we've got till it's gone. That's so true, especially when it comes to toilet paper.

Don't you hate it when you stock up on big bags of the best full-sized candy bars, but no trick or treaters come to your house? Next year, I'll be the cool neighbor who gives out Jell-O shots and Jaeger Bombs.

Back in the day, my girlfriend broke up with me because I stole her wheelchair. I didn't worry about it. I knew she'd come crawling back.

IRS call: "Thank you for your continued patience. Please remain on the line and one of our representatives will be with you shortly. In the meantime, please enjoy our complimentary Muzak, fully distorted to increase your anxiety."

My parents love each other eternally, yet bicker constantly. It's a daily grudge match, and there are no rules. If I recorded them, I could create the greatest American sitcom of all time.

I asked my wife, Sally, why she never blinks during foreplay. She answered, "There's never enough time."

The best holiday gift for your parents isn't in a store. It's in your heart, and you need to deliver it in person.

I just read that an OB/GYN has to go to school for twelve to fifteen years before they can get into that business. That's a lot of hard work. Back in high school, after a Friday night football game, I got into that business with no training at all.

Names matter. In the sixties and seventies, there was a highly successful little square chocolate candy appetite suppressant called AIDS. Then the eighties came along, and their business collapsed when suddenly, nobody wanted AIDS anywhere near their mouths.

You see these shoes? I bought them from a drug dealer. I don't know what he laced them with, but I've been tripping all day.

My wife and I were spying on my teenage son's browser history. It was full of sadomasochistic porn. Horrified, my wife exclaimed, "Oh my God, what are we going to do?" So I said, "We're sure as hell not going to spank him!"

I have always dreamed of being really big somewhere. Next month, I'm moving to Tokyo.

I believe that eyebrows, ear hairs, and nose hairs are in a "let's see who can embarrass him the most" contest.

I believe a Bohemian is one who lives an artistic lifestyle, placing freedom of self-expression above all other desires, including wealth, social conformity, and status. So, I'm not just a slob.

My friend Randy and I were having an argument. He said, "Pat, I'm recently divorced, so I don't need *you* telling me to go fuck myself!"

You're in the service industry. You work hard. You take care of yourself. Your customers depend on you. You take pride in your work. The pay is good. The hours are long and hard—but you knew that when you got into prostitution.

American politics would be hilarious if the fate of the world didn't hang in the balance.

I believe that if you stay in one place long enough, you're liable to get something named after you. It could be a street, a building, a bridge, or, for the lucky few, a disease.

Back in my twenties, I knew this extremely pissed-off little guy. Every time I saw him, he was angry as hell. His last name was Head and his first name was Richard, but everyone called him Dick.

I made it to the final round on *Jeopardy*. The last clue: "Two things found in cells." Thirty seconds. That silly music. With four seconds left, I wrote: "Blacks and Mexicans."

With the slightest breeze, my dog will lie down on his back, feet in the air, spread eagle, with his junk hangin' out. But if I do it, I get a lifetime ban from Chuck E. Cheese.

Have you seen my wife? I think she might be dead. The sex is the same, but the dishes are really piling up.

Caucasians need to step it up in the color game. *White* is so boring. Suggestions are as follows: pinky-white, ivory-white, limestone-white, freckledy-white, marble-white. I know a woman who is so white that if this were the early eighties, I'd probably try to snort her.

Don't bother walking a mile in my shoes; that would be boring. Spend thirty seconds inside my head—that'll freak you right out.

Some people hate change. But change is what this ride called life is all about. I say ride the wave or get off the surfboard.

I came, I saw, I forgot what the hell I was doing. I retraced my steps, I got lost, now I need to pee.

If God made man in his image and likeness, why aren't we all invisible?

A man in a bar turns to the woman next to him and says, "Hey, I heard an interesting stat the other day. They said that 80 percent of women masturbate in the shower. Know what the other 20 percent do?"
"No, what?" she asks.
The man replies, "Yeah, I figured you were in the first group."

I told myself it's time to quit drinking. But I'm not about to start listening to some drunk guy's advice.

I believe that hitting the gym is a wonderful way to make your slow, inevitable march to death a little more attractive.

I figure the ultimate form of rejection must be when your hand falls asleep while rubbing one out.

When I won, I got so excited, I threw the game ball into the crowd. Apparently, that's not the best way to celebrate a victory in bowling.

In our oh-so-sensitive politically correct world, I'm not fat; I'm gravitationally challenged.

Horny, I asked my wife if she wanted to try a new position tonight. In a sexy voice, she responded, "Oh, yes, baby. You stand over there by the ironing board, and I'll sit on the couch, drinking beer and farting."

When he was five years old, my son wrote a letter to Santa. He asked the Jolly One to bring him a little brother for Christmas. Two weeks later, my son received a response from the North Pole. It said, "Send me your mommy."

You know that Japanese thing where you tidy up your life by getting rid of the possessions that don't bring you joy? So far, I've thrown out cauliflower, kale, the bathroom scale, the treadmill, and the cable bill. I feel better already.

Everything happens for a reason. Sometimes the reason is you're stupid and make bad decisions.

When you love what you do, it's fun, and you completely lose track of the time. You know what makes me completely lose track of the time? Sleep.

Obligatory cheesehead joke: How do you get a Wisconsin woman on an elevator? Grease her hips and throw in a Twinkie.

People who have never lived in LA think it's always summer in Southern California. The Beach Boys lied. It's not. Los Angeles actually has four distinct seasons: fire, mudslide, drought, and monsoon. You're thinking I left out earthquakes. I didn't. Earthquakes are not a season; they're a constant.

I want what we all want: less traffic, more parking spaces, shorter checkout lines, and fewer assholes. So, when the hell is that damned Rapture?

Breaking news: A nine-year old girl has disappeared after using a moisturizing cream that makes you look ten years younger. In other news …

What's up with that circle dance dogs do? Three circles, squat, drop, kick dirt everywhere. And why does my other dog rush in to inspect the spot, sniff it, then cover it with his pee? Is there a name for this?

For some reason, every time I see a kissing scene in a movie, I hear a toddler slurping Jell-O off a plastic spoon.

Two nuns are riding bicycles down a cobbled street. The first nun says, "I've never come this way before"; the second nun replies, "Must be the cobbles."

I saw this sign in the window of a bookstore that was going out of business. It said, "Sorry, no public restrooms. Try Amazon!"

CBD oil really does make your pains disappear. But for that really big pain in the ass, you'll need a restraining order.

"Did you hear about Elizabeth? She had triplets, and then two weeks later, she had twins!"
"That's impossible; how did it happen?"
"One of her triplets was kidnapped!"

I don't believe life is like a box of chocolates. To me, life is like a roll of toilet paper. The closer you get to the end, the faster it goes.

I went to the dentist yesterday. He gave me helium. I said, "Helium? How does that deaden the pain?" He said, "It doesn't, but when you scream, it'll be freakin' hilarious."

I'm a sensitive guy. I love women. I understand their struggle. I'd never tell a woman how to dress, who to friend, or what to think. But how to vote?

I am really upset over the weight I've gained in the last few years. In fact, I'm flabbergasted.

As a kid, I got in a lot of trouble. In grade school, my butt was set on fire regularly by the nuns. In high school, I was suspended four times and expelled once. What's the moral of the story? Hell if I know, but I can tell you this:

sometimes you have to take chances and break a few rules to have the kind of fun worth remembering.

If you're an adult and you're eating Froot Loops right out of the box in the middle of the day and you don't live in your parents' basement, please share with me the phone number of your weed dealer.

Things have gotten so bad, women have started donating their eggs. They get $15,000–$20,000 for them! Men can donate their sperm for cash. They get a hundred bucks—or arrested.

Why does the bar association prohibit sex between a lawyer and a client? So the client doesn't get billed twice for the same thing.

I believe that if the whole world smoked a joint at the same time, there would be world peace for at least two hours. Followed by a global food shortage.

Let me get this straight. You have chosen to treat your body like a temple? Where's the fun in that? I treat mine like Mardi Gras. *Laissez les bon temps rouler.*

I've gotten out of bed every morning for sixty years. That's roughly 21,360 sit-ups and not a single ab to show for it.

My boss came to work this morning in a brand-new Lamborghini. He saw me admiring it, so he gave me a little advice. He said, "If you work hard, keep your nose to the grindstone, burn the midnight oil, and do your best every day, I'll get a second one of these next year."

As a kid, *Sesame Street* taught me the importance of education, empathy, and kindness. Bugs Bunny taught me that revenge on my enemies must be quick, clever, and brutal.

My buddy died when I couldn't remember his blood type. As he died, he kept telling me to "be positive," but it's hard without him. On the brighter side, I now have an EpiPen. He gave it to me right before he died. It seemed important to him that I have it.

I was hanging out with my buddies at The Station Grille, a local dive bar that we love. We were all shocked to see a girl get her nipple pierced right in front of us. That's when I shouted, "Oh my God, I suck at darts!"

On our first date, I asked Julie, "How do you like it?"
Julie answered quickly, "Doggie style, with you slapping my ass and pulling my hair."
I thought about that for a moment, then I said, "Good to know, but I was talking about the wine."

In the Garden of Eden, Adam asked God why He made Eve so beautiful.
God responded, "I made Eve beautiful so you will always love her."
Then Adam asked, "Then why did you make Eve so dumb?"
God responded, "I made Eve dumb so she will always love you."

Jimmy went to the bookstore and asked the young female assistant,
"Do you have the new book out for men with short penises?"
The young girl said, "I'm not sure if it's in yet."
Jimmy said, "That's the one. I'll take it."

I'm in mourning. I lost a good friend and drinking buddy last Saturday night in a tragic accident. Yeah, he got his finger caught in a wedding ring.

Social media has made it possible for me to get drunk at home alone and still make a total ass of myself in public.

It's been a crazy weird day. First, I found a hat full of money. Then I got chased down the street by some lunatic with a guitar.

I believe you can be outrageous. You can even be naughty. And people will love you, as long as your outrageous naughtiness has at its heart kindness.

I just won ten bucks in the Mega Millions Lottery Jackpot. Please respect our privacy as my family tries to decide the next step forward in this exciting and pivotal time in our lives.

Two facts: One: Sixty-three Earths can fit inside Uranus. Two: There will never be a time in my life when fact number one doesn't make me laugh.

If you meet a woman who admits she's wrong, apologizes, and changes her ways—that's not a woman; that's a man. Women don't do that.

It was after midnight when my phone rang. It was my best friend, and he said he didn't know what to do. He loved his girlfriend, but she just started smoking. I said, "First of all, slow down, and then apply more lube."

I'm a bourbon enthusiast. The more bourbon I drink, the more enthusiastic I get.

It was my first high school dance. I was a shy freshman, but I mustered up the courage to approach a beautiful cheerleader and ask, "Will you dance with me?"
Laughing, the cheerleader scoffed, "I'm not going to dance with a baby."
I was shocked, so I immediately apologized rather loudly. "I am so sorry; I didn't realize you were pregnant."

My grandfather tried to warn them about the Titanic. He screamed and shouted about the iceberg and how the ship was going to sink, but all they did was throw him out of the theater.

I love Facebook. It keeps us connected to people we never really knew and never plan to see again. Plus, it's America's great equalizer. It's the only place in the world where one man's doctorate in constitutional law from Harvard is equal to another man's fifth-grade education.

What do you call someone who speaks two languages? Bilingual. What do you call someone who speaks three languages? Trilingual. What do you call someone who only speaks one language? American.

I bought a pack of condoms at Walgreens. As I paid for them, the cashier asked, "Do you need a bag?" I said, "Nah, she's not that ugly."

If you can't pee off your own back porch, your neighbors are too damn close.

If I refuse to turn my clocks back in the fall, will I be living in the future?

A child's worst nightmare begins with these words: "Your mom and I have something we'd like to discuss with you."

Gay marriage was finally legalized in America. If recreational pot becomes legal in all states, one part of the Book of

Leviticus will finally make sense: "A man who lays with another man should be stoned."

I was in the lobby of a high-rise building looking for the suite number for my recording session. Random guy walked up to me and said, "Is that your real hair?" Startled, I said, "I can assure you, my hair is real. However, the beer belly is a prosthesis." He didn't get it.

Little Red Riding Hood was walking through the forest on the way to visit her grandmother, when suddenly the Big Bad Wolf jumped out from behind a tree and yelled, "Aha! Now I've got you, and I'm gonna eat you!"
"Eat, eat, eat!" screamed Little Red Riding Hood. "Dammit! Doesn't anybody screw anymore?"

This morning, the cute weather girl on TV said, "Plenty of sunshine heading our way!" So I sang, "Zippity doo dah, zippity ay!"

This friend of mine is a vegan. She said that I can't possibly be a real animal lover because I eat meat and that if I really loved them, I would only eat vegetables and grains. So I said, "If you really loved animals, you'd stop eating all their damned food."

Some folks hear voices. Others see people who aren't there. The rest have no imagination whatsoever.

My good friend Rob told me about a beautiful young woman who lives in the apartment beneath him who enjoys sunbathing in the nude.
He said, "I am like a god to her."
I said, "How so?"
He replied, "Because I'm always watching over her, and so far, she's never seen me."

Not to be a crotchety old man, but I believe that if you watched an evening of the pre-teen-oriented shows on the Disney Channel, you would come to the conclusion that not only should abortion be legal; it should also be retroactive. Now, get off my lawn!

My whole world really sucks right now. That's a good thing. If it didn't, I'm pretty sure we would all fall off.

I've noticed that more and more these days people are turning away from the church and going back to God.

Tell someone you love them today, because life is short. But shout it at them in German, because life is also terrifying and confusing.

I remain an eternal optimist. I dream of a better world where chickens can cross the road without having their motives questioned.

Here's a question for all my essential-oil friends: which essential oil calms angry, belligerent family members? Chloroform? It's chloroform, isn't it?

If you think that you are smarter than the previous generation, fifty years ago, the owner's manual of a car showed you how to adjust the valves. Today, it warns you not to drink the contents of the battery.

When I offer to wash your back in the shower, all you have to say is yes or no. Not all this, "Who are you, and how did you get in here?" nonsense.

Two friends are fishing together when one turns to the other and asks, "Is it rape if it's your wife?"

The second man casts his line and responds, "No, I don't think so."

"What a relief," says the first man. "I thought you'd be mad as hell!"

It's really cool that last names tell us so much about old family professions. Like the Smith family, they were all blacksmiths. The Bowman family, they were all archers. And the Dickinson family, they were all in prison.

Back when we were married, my first wife told me, "For Father's Day, I'm going to make you the happiest man in the world." I said, "Fantastic, but I think the kids will miss you."

Three conspiracy theorists walked into a bar. You can't tell me that was just a coincidence.

I don't understand why drunk me always thinks he has more money than sober me.

If you're going to break up with your girlfriend, do it in a fancy restaurant. That way if she starts crying, the patrons will assume you just proposed to her, and they'll all stand and applaud.

What's the difference between a dog and a fox? Four martinis.

I might wake up early and go for a five-mile run, or I might wake up and be a lottery winner. Either way, the odds are about the same.

I'll admit it; I love to watch cooking shows. They inspire me to order delivery.

My ex owned a parakeet. Oh my God, the damned thing would never shut up. But the bird was cool.

Have you ever noticed that if you wear the same shirt long enough, it becomes an adult bib?

If I can hear you chew, I have already fantasized about your death.

The secret to a good marriage is honesty. If you can fake that, you'll have a happy wife.

Two stoners are walking down a railroad track. One stoner says, "Man, this is a really long staircase!" The other stoner says, "Man, I don't mind the stairs; it's the low handrail that's killing me."

At Christmas time, there's nothing I love more than sitting in front of a roaring fire, sipping a good bourbon, and singing Christmas carols. That's probably why I'm no longer a fireman.

I wrote a joke that got me arrested by the PC Police. When I got out of jail, I punched a black guy and got arrested again for impersonating a police officer.

Sex without love is a meaningless experience, but as far as meaningless experiences go, it's one of the best.

Our family doctor called last week to tell me my wife was in the hospital. I asked if she was going to be all right. He said, "I'm quite concerned; I'm afraid she's critical." I replied, "Don't worry, Doc; she's always like that."

In the back of the ambulance, the EMT asks the patient, "Can you describe the snake that bit you?" The patient answers, "Yes, yes, I can. It was like an angry rope!"

What do you say to a drummer in a three-piece suit? "Will the defendant please rise?"

If you want to change the world, you better do it while you're single. Once you're married, you won't even be allowed to change the TV channel.

It's a shame that nothing is built in America anymore. I just got a new big-screen TV. On the back, it says, *built-in antenna*. I don't even know where Antenna is.

Her body tensed and quivered as she felt wave after wave surge through her. I guess I should have told her about my new electric fence.

Today, I spotted an albino Dalmatian. It was the least I could do for her.

The guys at the gym call me a fat loser; it's really great how they notice my efforts.

Sure, silence is golden, right up to the point where you're handcuffed in the back of a windowless van on your way to prison.

I walked into Bar Louie to wet my whistle. I saw a beautiful, well-dressed woman sitting on a barstool alone. I walked up to her and said, "Hi there. How's it going tonight?"
She turned to me, looked me straight in the eyes, and said, "I'll screw anybody anytime, anywhere, any place; it doesn't matter to me."
I raised one eyebrow and said, "No kidding? What law firm do you work for?"

At first, we had empires, run by emperors; then we had kingdoms, run by kings—and now we have countries ...

My teenage daughter came home from school in a rage. "I had sex-education class in school today, and Daddy! You lied to me! You told me if I had sex before my sixteenth birthday, my boyfriend would die!" I put down the gun I was cleaning and calmly said, "Oh, he will, sweetheart; he will."

In Japan, they have great respect for family, especially the elderly. In America, most of us only care about family when it's too late to do anything about it.

My wife was furious at me for kicking dropped ice cubes under the refrigerator. I told her not to worry about it; it's just water under the fridge. (*Groan*)

When I was a kid, cities were safe, and there was a phone booth on every corner. Now the phone booths are gone, and cities are dangerous. No phone booth, no Superman.

I like food. Obviously. But I wanted to pay more for it, get less of it, and make it a lot less tasty. So I went gluten free. I was determined to succeed—I stuck with my new plan for an entire seventeen minutes.

I didn't realize how bad a driver I was until that female voice on my GPS said, "In four hundred feet, pull to the right, stop, and let me the hell out."

It was our first date, and as we were filling each other in on our pasts, I said, "A genie once gave me the option of having a longer penis or a better memory." Curious, my date asked, "And which did you choose?" I replied, "I don't remember."

Sometimes, someone comes into our lives out of nowhere, makes our hearts race, and changes our lives forever. We call these people cops.

Inside every elderly person is a seventeen-year-old kid who just wants to know what the hell happened.

An old man and an old lady are getting ready for bed one night when all of a sudden, the woman bursts out of the bathroom, flings open her robe, and yells, "Super pussy!" The old man says, "I'll have the soup."

Money problems, cheating, or sheer boredom have long been enough to wreck a marriage. But today, it seems most couples break up because they begin seeking sunshine in different directions.

Why don't lawyers go to the beach? Cats keep trying to bury them.

You wanna know what my New Year's resolution is? I resolved to stop being friends with people who want to know what my New Year's resolution is.

I just saw a print ad for an "Improvised Shakespeare Company." Great idea. The problem with Shakespeare has always been the writing.

We should all be extremely offended when rich guys lose a lot of money and commit suicide. That means they'd rather be dead than live like us.

---

eHarmony claims that they match people on thirty-four levels. Who the hell has thirty-four levels? I have, maybe, three levels. They are: the once-handsome but rapidly declining outer shell; the inner world of conflicts, lies, and heartbreaks; and my sphincter. And there are cameras for two of those.

The Cleveland Browns. If you can't say something nice, don't say anything at all. Okay, I'll play. Here goes. After watching the Browns struggle through so many losing seasons, I examined their efforts on the field, and I found nothing offensive.

Time travel is real. If you want to experience what life was like fifty years ago, take a trip to Branson, Missouri.

———————

I believe that with the sound turned down, it is impossible to tell the difference between a commercial for jewelry and a commercial for Viagra. Though one often leads to the other.

———————

A one-armed stoner climbed a tree and became too frightened to climb back down. So I said to the gathering crowd, "Getting him down is easy. First, get his attention. Second, smile at him. And third, everybody wave!"

———————

Next time a couple comes up to me in public and the wife says, "Don't I know you from somewhere? Are you on TV?" I'll say, "No, but I am on a bunch of videos. Hi, my name is Rod Steele." (I shake their hands vigorously.) "I'm a porn star. Want my autograph?"

———————

I was having a hard time falling asleep. I was tired of counting sheep. So I decided to count endangered species. Damn, I ran out.

———————

There's nothing like the Christmas-morning joy on my child's face when he sees the shiny new PlayStation box I got him containing three pairs of socks.

When I was a newlywed, I arrived home one night with a big bouquet of flowers. My wife, the gymnast, met me at the door. Upon seeing the bouquet, she stripped, dropped to the floor, did a handstand, and spread her legs. In a sexy voice, she moaned, "This is for the flowers!" I scoffed, "Don't be silly. I'm sure we have a vase around here somewhere."

Child: "Mom, am I ugly?" Mother: "I told you not to call me Mom in public!"

When it comes to the gods of other religions, we are all atheists.

My belly button is actually a scar left from a knife fight I got into with a guy wearing a mask after I was evicted from my first home. And I still don't know why he slapped my ass.

I don't always diet, but when I do, I expect the results to be instant, dramatic, and spectacular.

A priest is walking through town at his new parish when a hooker approaches him.

"Blow jobs for twenty dollars if you're interested."

Confused by this, he smiles, blesses her, and goes back to the church. He sees one of the nuns and asks her, "Sister, what's a blow job?"

She replies, "Twenty bucks. Same as in town."

Grab a handful of sand, close your fist around it, and squeeze it as tight as you can. The sand slips right through your fingers. The same is true with parenting a child. Hold on loosely, never give up, and never completely let go.

Becoming a parent is fantastic. It's a truly rewarding experience. Almost as good as not becoming one.

The NFL: making men forget tomorrow is Monday since 1920.

Why am I laughing? I just heard a new parent say that they believe parenting will be a lot easier when their child gets older.

Going to a burger joint for a salad is like going to a hooker for a hug.

I see people my age out there climbing mountains and zip lining through jungles, and here I am feeling good about myself because I got one leg through my underwear without losing my balance.

Two eggs are boiling in a pot on the stove. One says, "I've got a huge crack." The other replies, "Stop teasing; I'm not even hard yet!"

When I was in college, I had a 4.0 GPA, made the Dean's List, and was the valedictorian, all while working two full-time jobs. And I learned that anything is possible—if you lie.

When I dunk my cookies in a glass of milk, I always think of you. Then I hold them under until the bubbles stop.

I woke up hungover to the sound of my neighbor mowing his lawn. I thought, *Screw him; he's just gonna have to mow around me.*

I'm the best man at my buddy's third wedding. Is it appropriate to open my speech at the rehearsal dinner with, "Welcome back, everybody"?

Our marriage counselor said I need to treat my wife the way I treated her on our first date. So, after dinner tonight, I'm gonna drop her off at her parents' house.

If women are always right, why do they keep choosing the wrong men?

I believe the first guy to discover milk did a lot of other weird shit too. And don't get me started on the first guy to eat oysters.

My brother was always quick with a joke. One morning, we were talking on the phone when he exclaimed, "Oh my God!" Worried, I asked, "What happened?" He whispered reverently, "I just dropped a deuce that was so big, it could have applied for statehood."

The grass is always greener on the other side of the fence because my neighbor doesn't have my dogs.

Studies prove our number-one fear is speaking in public, and our number-two fear is death. That means when we go to a funeral, we'd rather be in the casket than giving the eulogy.

It's a proven fact that the fastest way to a man's wallet is through his heart.

Barber, hairdresser, whatever you call them, tip them well. Because they can leave your DNA at a crime scene.

As I began methodically working on the second sleeve, I thought, *They must put crack in Girl Scout cookies.*

Feeling blue? You could drown yourself, but don't. Simply remind yourself that today's difficulties are but a ripple in the stream of all good things.

I like female dogs. When you scratch their bellies, there's no kickstand.

I believe relationships are based on science. Love is a matter of chemistry, and sex is a matter of physics.

The most embarrassed I have ever been in my entire life was when my parents caught me watching a hard-core lesbian sex video ... over their shoulders.

Satan rehabbed hell to make it even more horrific. He replaced the hot coals with Legos.

The following is the complete list of condescending jerks on the internet I wish would shut the hell up: vegans.

The nuns were right about a lot of things, but they were wrong about me. I did not go blind.

I can quit drinking anytime I want. I've done it hundreds of times.

The true spirit of the Christmas season is alive in every Black Friday brawl.

My wife told me that sex is better on a Hawaiian vacation. Worst postcard I've ever received.

Effective TV commercials increase product sales. I believe there should be an award for the copywriter whose words move the most product. That award should go every year to the person who wrote, "If your erection lasts more than four hours ..."

Karma Sutra is when fate screws you in every way possible.

Do you know the difference between a circus and the Miss America beauty pageant? Well, one is a cunning array of stunts.

My wife and I went to the homeowners' association meeting last night. They were discussing fire prevention. The woman running the meeting asked the crowd, "What steps would you take if your house were to catch on fire?" I shouted, "Big freakin' steps!"

Your career is over when you decide you are done kissing ass ... also applies to your marriage.

After-Christmas return policies are strict. It was the first week of January. I had the receipt and everything. But Walmart still wouldn't refund what I paid for that damned tree.

Have you ever sneezed so hard that you farted and peed a little? Yeah, me neither.

There's a driving force in my life that inspires me every morning to jump out of bed and greet the new day. It's my bladder.

When a politician says tax cuts are aimed at the middle class, I say, "Yeah, like a loaded gun."

I have enochlophobia; it's the fear of crowds. There are thousands who share my phobia. So I joined their big support group. When do we meet? Never.

Stoners are the world's most careful drivers. They never run stop signs. They come to a complete stop and patiently wait for them to turn green.

Have you ever won an argument on Facebook? Me neither.

The Waffle House is the perfect place for late-night stoners and drunks. It's the only restaurant chain in the world with a "point and grunt" menu.

There is only one business that allows a partner to bankrupt it, abscond with all the assets, and leave the other partner paying for everything as if the business were still in operation. That business is called marriage.

I need to cut back on sugar and work out. If I were murdered today, the police chalk line would be a circle.

Somehow, I managed to hear this conversation between a beer bottle, a mirror, and a condom:
The beer bottle: "You break me, and you'll get a year of bad luck!"
The mirror: "You kiddin' me? You break me, and you'll get seven years of bad luck!"
The condom just walked away, laughing.

There is more money being spent on breast implants and Viagra today than on Alzheimer's research. This means that in 20 years, there will be a huge elderly population with perky boobs, huge erections, and absolutely no idea what to do with them.

A sure sign that you're past your prime is when your wife says, "Honey, let's run upstairs and make love!" and your answer is, "Baby, you choose, 'cause I sure as hell can't do both!"

I was sitting at the bar having drinks with my old buddy Matt, and we were discussing our wives.

He asked me, "Do you and your wife ever do it doggie style?"

I answered, "Well, not exactly. She's more into the trick-dog aspect of it."

Matt responded, "Oh, I see. Kinda kinky, huh?"

I said, "Well, not exactly. I sit up and beg, and she rolls over and plays dead."

This observation is for my dear, sweet brother: If you live in the hearts of those you leave behind, you never die. And he does, and he always will.

My penis is always going, "She's hot, man. You gotta git you some of that!" My brain always answers, "No way, little guy. I respect women, and I refuse to objectify them." I swear, sometimes my penis can be a real dick.

Love, honor, and obey? Be happy if you find someone you're comfortable staring at phones with.

Vegans, always complaining. "That animal was tortured. He suffered and was killed for you." Yeah? So was Jesus, and nobody's complaining about that.

You see guys take a newspaper or magazine into the john. Some go in there with their smartphones. But nobody ever goes in there with a Hershey bar.

I believe that working from home is freedom. It's also less laundry, fewer showers, sweatpants, and a beard.

The best thing about a king-size bed is the demilitarized zone.

We would have world peace if Superman had saved our world as often as "delete history" has saved mine.

Hey guys, you wanna know the secret to getting your wife hot and excited? Tell her to calm down.

I don't take chances that would risk my life. The closest I've ever gotten to bungee jumping was the day I was born.

Texting: a communication method invented to guarantee that its users' conversations are devoid of any trace of honest emotion or intimacy.

Two shrinks meet at their twentieth college reunion. One of them looks like he just graduated—young, fit, and trim. The other one looks ragged, weathered, and old. The older-looking shrink is taken aback. "How do you do it? What's your secret? Listening to people's problems day in and day out, year after year, has taken a terrible toll on me." The younger-looking shrink replies, "Who listens?"

There are all kinds of laws: laws of mathematics, chemistry, momentum, thermodynamics—but gravity? It's a real downer. (*Groan*)

Some guys really enjoy doing drugs. Eventually, they lose their cars, houses, kids, money, and health. Don't do drugs. Get married, same result.

A lot of guys say, "I really worked my butt off today!" That's not funny, but it would be if it were true.

I have questions. Do cranberries ever get urinary tract infections?

I don't know how cats do it. Nine lives? Who pays for all those funerals?

I have finally realized that we are indeed getting older. Friends, now is a good time to tell all the people in your life how you feel about them. Don't wait until you're on your deathbed. You might be too weak to lift your middle finger.

I've decided to donate my body to science. I know this will make my dad happy. He always wanted me to go to medical school.

After years of complaining about how stupid their parents are, kids will be surprised to discover that the older they get, the smarter their parents get.

I was at the customer-service desk, returning a pair of jeans that were too tight. "Was anything wrong with them?" the clerk asked. "Yes," I said. "They hurt my feelings."

When I was a little kid, my parents would always say, "Excuse my French," after they cursed. That's why I'll never forget my first day of school, when the teacher asked the class if any of us knew any French.

Am I the only one who believes a better name for *nose* would be *schnozzle*? "Honey, where's my neti pot? I need to douche my schnozzle."

I believe Sazerac is a clever use of onomatopoeia. It's the last call, end of the night, white-flag surrender, and spew of another bro on Bourbon Street.

Judging by the leftover Halloween candy, kids don't like Mars bars. Apparently, they have never tried one with a shot of Jack.

Horny? Addicted to porn? There is a cure. Watch a seventies-era adult film. Those hairy apes will make you forget ever liking any of it.

For all the guys who don't have my wit, gift of gab, or magnetic personality, I remain overweight. I consider it a public service.

My bologna doesn't have a first name. My bologna doesn't have a second name. My bologna is the cheap store brand.

Last week, my wife, Sally, asked me to get her lipstick out of her purse. I accidentally handed her a glue stick. She's still not talking to me.

I'm a bit of a hermit. I'm not antisocial; I'm just allergic to stupidity.

At twelve, my daughter Natalie was an avid reader. She loved books. She had the entire Nancy Drew collection. One December, I asked her what she wanted for Christmas. She said, "I'd love to get a nice bookmark." I immediately burst into tears. Why? She's my daughter, she's twelve years old, and she doesn't know me. She thinks my name is Mark.

When a close-talking bore has you cornered at a party and you feel trapped, there is one surefire way to escape. Tell them you just sharted yourself and run.

I don't get it. When you have a loved one cremated, it's a respectful way to say goodbye. But if you do the same thing at home, it's called "destroying the evidence."

When your best friend is about to marry the wrong woman, let him. Why should you have all the fun?

Did you hear about that new restaurant that opened last week? It's called Karma. It's really different. There's no menu. You get what you deserve.

I can tell a lot about people by what music they listen to or what books they read. There is a better, totally foolproof test. Everything you need to know about someone is revealed in a restaurant when you see how they treat the wait staff.

Why is it that when I'm driving, I can't find where I'm going until I turn the music down?

What's it like to have six-pack abs? Hell if I know. But I can tell you exactly what it's like to have beer-keg abs.

I'm no expert on preparing for retirement, but I've got a friend who is still waiting for a magic fairy riding a unicorn to fly in on a rainbow made of stardust to save him.

After a long bout with stomach flu, I am attempting solid food for the first time in a week and must further report that I am not yet cocky enough to fart.

Science newsflash for vegans: vegetables are alive and have feelings too, so stop killing them. If you're really concerned about all living beings, try eating rocks or dirt. They don't feel a thing.

Ever since the unemployment rate hit an all-time low, many Americans have had a hard time finding a decent-paying third job.

Making love after the age of ninety is like shooting pool with a rope.

When a woman sees a messy toilet, she thinks, *Gotta clean that up immediately.* When a man sees a messy toilet, he thinks, *Target practice.*

Civilized society has a minimum requirement for anyone over eighteen, and that is to call your parents at least once a week.

It's a little-known historical fact that all Egyptian pharaohs were buried with their hands crossed over their chests because it was a popular belief that in the afterlife, there would be countless water slides.

A politician's oath: "I promise to tell the lie, the whole lie, and nothing but the lie ... *so help me.*"

Employers who don't pay worth a damn expect workers to stand on one foot, bend over backward, and do a cartwheel to kiss their asses.

My optometrist just told me that I'm color-blind. His diagnosis came completely out of the purple.

My wife and I have decided that we do not want to have children. If anybody does, please private message me your address and we'll drop ours off tomorrow.

I'm so proud of myself. Yesterday, I tried on some clothes I haven't worn in ten years. They fit like a glove. Okay, it was a pair of gloves.

Divorce-court judge: "Mr. Duke, I have reviewed your case very carefully and have decided to give your wife $3,000 a month." So I said, "Thank you; that's very fair of you, Your Judgeship. And every now and then, I'll try to kick in a few bucks myself."

I will gladly climb a mountain, crawling on hands and knees over hot coals, through broken glass and barbed wire, to get to a good single-malt scotch.

You know you're over the hill when you start having dry dreams and wet farts.

When I hear muffled laughter coming from my bathroom mirror, it is spooky, it is weird, and it is time to diet.

Don't tell anyone, because I haven't copyrighted it yet. But I have created an invention that is guaranteed to make every woman happy. Can you keep a secret? Okay. I invented a chocolate-flavored dildo that ejaculates money.

I realize that some of you might be offended by my jokes. So please tweet your angry responses on your smartphone made by a six-year-old in China.

My definition of an intellectual is someone who can hear Wagner's "Ride of the Valkyries" and not sing, "Kill da wabbit!"

This morning, Jesus spoke to me. He said, "Looking at the mess Christians have made of my world sure makes me glad I'm a Jew!"

I know I joke a lot, but now I'm serious, and I'm asking you to wish me good luck. Today, I'm thrilled because I have a meeting at the bank. If it goes well, I'll be able to pay off my credit cards and student loans and be completely debt free. I'm so excited, I'm having trouble putting on my ski mask.

I went to the doctor because I'm overweight. He said, "If you don't lose weight starting right now, you're gonna die." I said, "Doc, thanks for your honesty, but I don't believe that's gonna be enough motivation."

What's the difference between a slut and a bitch? A slut will have sex with anyone, and a bitch will have sex with anyone but you.

Maybe tear ducts are Mother Nature's wiper blades in a storm. All I know is that a man who cries sees the world more clearly.

The next time a friend hands you their baby to hold, you should say, "No thanks; I'm a vegetarian."

Tequila and I are not a good combination. One of us disappears, and the other one winds up naked.

My new joke book should be coming out soon, and I sincerely regret having eaten it.

Do you suffer from shyness? Do you sometimes wish you were more assertive? Ask your doctor or pharmacist about tequila.

Back in the days before the internet, movies, television, radio, and the light bulb were invented, what did they do at night for entertainment? I don't know, but they sure had a lot of kids.

It seems like the poorest people I know are the ones with the most money.

Last year in America, 1,587 men died while lifting weights in the gym. During that same period, only eleven men died while drinking scotch. Make wise choices, my friends.

At breakfast, my wife brought up the fact that my hair was too long and I now have man boobs. She asked, "Have you ever been mistaken for a woman?" I said, "No. Have you?"

There is a big difference between a *quiet* woman and a *silent* woman. The first one is a miracle. The second is a time bomb.

Crazy ex-girlfriends are like a box of chocolates. They will kill your dog.

A man walks into a lawyer's office and inquires about the rates. "Five hundred and fifty dollars for three questions," replies the lawyer. "Isn't that awfully steep?" asks the man. "Yes," the lawyer replies, "and what's your third question?"

At dinner one night, my soon-to-be ex said, "I'm having an affair." Handing the menu back to the waiter, I said, "I'll have the same."

When a friend proudly produces a loud fart, I don't say, "Nice one." That would be rude. I start singing "Like a Virgin."

I went to my high school reunion. I didn't recognize anybody, so I left. On the way home, I kept wondering, *Who the hell were all those crippled, gray, bald, fat, old people?* Then I saw myself in the rearview mirror.

As a little kid, I was told I had a medical condition that could only be cured by eating a tablespoon of dirt every day. I survived that malady and thank my big brother, Johnny, for knowing how to cure it.

I announced on Facebook that spring had sprung and I was excited to go camping. I immediately got thousands of "likes" from mosquitoes.

My ex-wife's astrological sign was Cancer, and it's quite ironic how she died. She was beaten to death by a giant crab.

Time waits for no man, but every man is waiting for a woman.

I've got a kid in Africa that I feed, clothe, educate, and inoculate for seventy-five cents a day. Which is practically nothing compared to what it cost me to send him over there.

When my son was five, he got separated from me at a football game, so he went up to a policeman and said, "I've lost my dad!" "What's he like?" the cop inquired. My little boy said, "Scotch and porn!"

I am a white man. I possess great compassion, empathy, and open-minded, forward-thinking love for all. I am also clairvoyant. I know you stopped listening after, "I am a white man."

When I think about guys with Tourette syndrome, I often wonder what makes them tick.

A priest, a pedophile, and a rapist walk into a bar. He orders a drink.

I don't know about forcing all the guys in porn to wear condoms. But there is a strong case for goggles.

A blind man at Walmart is swinging his dog around on its leash like a helicopter. A shocked onlooker asks, "What the hell are you doing?" The blind man replies, "Oh, just lookin' around."

I was feeling lousy, so I went to my doctor to find out what was wrong. He said, "First, we're going to run some tests to see how your insurance reacts."

My kids never misquote me. In fact, they repeat word for word everything I wish I had never said.

I believe the difference between an oral thermometer and a rectal thermometer is most likely the taste.

A famous television Evangelist was checking into a swanky hotel. He stated rather loudly, "I hope the pornographic channels are disabled." The manager whispered, "No, it's regular porn, you sick bastard."

Once, I was watching a documentary about euthanasia with my ex. She asked, "If I get really sick, will you do that for me?" I answered, "Hell, I'll do that for you if you catch a cold!"

Okay, here is the beginning to the dumbest joke ever told: "Two guys walk into a bar ... "That's stupid. You know the second guy saw what the first guy did.

Speed kills, and nothing travels faster than bad news. Never share your personal problems online.

My nieces and nephews are so cute. So I bought tickets for all of us to see Disney on Ice. The ice was impressive, and Walt was extremely well preserved.

Here's the kind of joke I hate but can't resist: What did one saggy boob say to the other saggy boob? "If we don't get some support, people are gonna think we're nuts."

Politicians are always trying to bury us in bullshit, but we are like seeds. We grow in fertilizer.

What's a baby seal's least-favorite drink? Canadian Club on the rocks.

You know that feeling when you meet someone and your heart skips a beat? Yeah, that's arrhythmia. You can die from that.

A buddy of mine went to the eye doctor. In the middle of the exam, the doctor told him, "You really need to stop masturbating."
My friend replied, "Why, Doc? Am I going blind?"
The doctor said, "No, but you're really freaking out my nurse."

A blonde, a rabbi, and a lawyer walk into a bar. The bartender asks, "What is this, some kind of a joke?"

Every election season, I hear people say they want to put prayer back in our schools. All I can say is, as long as teachers are still giving exams, there will always be prayer in our schools.

If I had a dollar for every girl who found me unattractive, they would eventually find me attractive.

With age comes new skills. You can laugh, cough, sneeze, and pee all at the same time.

Rome wasn't built in a day. In the same vein, you don't get a body like mine overnight. It takes many years of dedicated neglect.

A herd of sheep threw a big holiday party. They were all crowded together. They couldn't decide what to do. Should they eat? Should they mingle? This party was a complete failure until the border collie showed up.

The only two types of business conducted successfully in a bar late at night are monkey and prostitution.

I called our family doctor to make an appointment and got the receptionist. "Good mornin'; I need to make an appointment."
She looked through the schedule and came back to me. "How does ten in the morning sound?"
I said, "Ten? No, that's way too many."

I never thought I would be the kind of person who wakes up early every morning to go exercise, and I was right.

"Hey Tom, long time no see. What have you been up to?" He whispered, "I've spent the last two years looking for my ex-wife's killer ... but no one will do it."

You know how when you buy one of those bags of salad and three days later, you pull it out of the refrigerator and the lettuce has started getting brown on the edges and there's a nasty liquid growing in the bottom of the bag? You know what doesn't do that? Cookies.

Life has never given me lemons. It has given me anger issues, anxiety attacks, a love for alcohol, and a serious dislike for assholes, but no lemons.

In English, "I love you." In French, *"Je t'aime."* In Spanish, *"Te amo."* In Alabama, "Nice tits; git in the truck."

If you're the smartest guy in the room, there's nothing for you there, so get the hell out—unless you're the teacher.

I used to live in Chicago. That town goes crazy on St. Patrick's Day. Well, I got "overserved," so I took a bus home. You probably think that was the safest thing for me to do. It wasn't. I've never driven a bus before.

If you really want to be a success in life, it's best to start out rich.

A woman ran up to me and yelled, "Give it to me right now!" Even more emphatically, she screamed, "I'm so wet I could scream!". So I said, "No way, lady. You are not getting my umbrella."

My wife yelled from upstairs, "Do you ever get a shooting pain in your chest like someone is sticking needles in a voodoo doll?" I answered no. She yelled, "How about now?"

Someone asked me what my plans were for the fall. It took me a moment to realize they were talking about autumn and not the collapse of civilization.

Leviticus is all about abominations and punishments. I believe it's time for an update. At the top of that list should be credit card companies, student loans, Big Pharma, and the IRS.

Did you hear about the dead lawyer who was too fat to fit in his coffin? They gave him an enema and buried him in a shoebox.

In life, as in business, you usually only have two moves: find your way or find your excuse.

Before deciding to have a child, there's one important question I believe you need to ask yourself: "Am I ready to watch the exact same cartoon on repeat for the next five years?"

If you are arrested and you have tattoos all over your face and neck, you are guilty as charged.

"Your mother cooks socks in hell!" –The Dyslexorcist

My friend Billy just told me his grandfather lived to be 102 years old and never used glasses. So I said, "I understand. You get drunk a lot quicker when you drink straight out of the bottle."

Flowers and balloons are now interchangeable for expressing our emotions at all the important events in our lives—except funerals.

A young couple go to bed with each other for the first time. She says, "I should warn you; I've got acute angina." He responds, "Your tits aren't bad either."

When you think about it, love and hate are two sides of the same coin. Indifference is the opposite of each.

LONG TOKES

A man is making dinner for his family. He's making deer, but he wants his kids to try it before they know what it is, fearful they may not give it a chance. He calls them to the dinner table.

At the table, the kids ask, "What is this?"

The father says, "Just try it."

The kids are stubborn and suspicious, so they ask again. "We aren't eating it until we know what it is, so what is it?"

The father says, "I'll give you a hint: it's what Mommy sometimes calls Daddy."

The youngest son screams, *"Don't eat it; it's a dick!"*

Last summer, I was walking along the beach in Santa Monica. I saw an ornate bottle that had washed up on shore. I picked it up, wiped the sand off of it, and damn if a genie didn't appear.

He said, "I will grant you three wishes, and for every wish granted, your ex will receive double."

"Okay, Mr. Genie, I want you to give me $1 billion and a luxury yacht."

"And your third wish?"

"My third wish is that you beat me half to death."

A biker stopped by the local Harley shop to have his bike fixed. They couldn't do it while he waited, so he said he didn't live far and would just walk home.

On the way home, he stopped at the hardware store and bought a bucket and an anvil. He stopped by the feed store and picked up a couple of chickens and a goose.

However, struggling outside the store, he now had a problem: how to carry all of his purchases home.

While he was scratching his head, he was approached by a little old lady, who told him she was lost. She asked, "Can you tell me how to get to 1603 Mockingbird Lane?"

The biker said, "Well, as a matter of fact, I live at 1616 Mockingbird Lane. I would walk you home, but I can't carry all this stuff."

The old lady suggested, "Why don't you put the anvil in the bucket, carry the bucket in one hand, put a chicken under each arm, and carry the goose in your other hand?"

"Why, thank you very much," he said and proceeded to walk the old girl home.

On the way, he said, "Let's take a shortcut and go down this alley. We'll be there in no time."

The little old lady looked him over cautiously and then said, "I am a lonely widow without a husband to defend me. How do I know that when we get in the alley, you won't hold me up against the wall, pull up my skirt, and have your way with me?"

The biker said, "Holy smokes, lady! I am carrying a bucket, an anvil, two chickens, and a goose. How in the world could I possibly hold you up against the wall and do that?"

The lady replied, "Set the goose down, cover him with the bucket, put the anvil on top of the bucket, and I'll hold the chickens."

A man goes to the doctor because he's having trouble moving his bowels. The doctor prescribes suppositories.
A week later, the guy goes back to his doctor and says, "These things aren't working. I still can't take a poop."
The doctor asks, "Are you sure you're taking them the right way?"
The man says, "Of course I'm sure. What do you expect me to do, shove them up my ass?"

I'm currently at the hospital. Today was just not a good day. I decided to go horseback riding with some friends, and it turned out to be a terrible mistake. I got on the horse and we started off slow, but before I knew it, the horse was at a full gallop, going as fast as he could possibly go. I couldn't hold on and I fell off—but my foot got caught in the stirrup, so the horse began dragging me! He wouldn't stop! The horse just kept going around and around in a circle. Thank goodness the store manager at Walmart came out and unplugged the machine.

Dear Tide:
I am writing to say what an excellent product you have. I've used it all my married life, as my mom always told me it was the best. Now that I am in my fifties, I find it even better!
In fact, about a month ago, I spilled some red wine on my new white blouse. My inconsiderate and uncaring husband started to belittle me about how clumsy I was and generally

THOUGHTS ON THE POT

started becoming a pain in the neck. One thing led to another, and somehow, I ended up with his blood on my new white blouse!

I grabbed my bottle of Tide with bleach alternative. To my surprise and satisfaction, all the stains came out! In fact, the stains came out so well that the detectives who came by yesterday told me that the DNA tests on my blouse were negative, and then my attorney called and said that I was no longer considered a suspect in the disappearance of my husband. What a relief! Going through menopause is bad enough without being a murder suspect!

I thank you, once again, for having a great product. Well, gotta go, I have to write to the Hefty bag people.

A young man named Chuck bought a horse from a farmer for $250. The farmer agreed to deliver the horse the next day. The next day, the farmer drove up to Chuck's house and said, "Sorry son, but I have some bad news. The horse died."

Chuck replied, "Well, then, just give me my money back."

The farmer said, "Can't do that. I went and spent it already."

Chuck said, "Okay, then just bring me the dead horse."

The farmer asked, "What ya gonna do with him?"

Chuck said, "I'm going to raffle him off."

The farmer said, "You can't raffle off a dead horse!"

Chuck said, "Sure I can. Watch me. I just won't tell anybody he's dead."

A month later, the farmer met up with Chuck and asked, "What happened with that dead horse?"

Chuck said, "I raffled him off. I sold five hundred tickets at five dollars apiece and made a profit of $2,495."
The farmer said, "Didn't anyone complain?"
"Just the guy who won. So I gave him his five dollars back."

After thirty-five years of marriage, a husband and wife came to see a therapist. When asked what the problem was, the wife went into a tirade listing every problem they had ever had in the years they had been married. It went on and on and on: neglect, lack of intimacy, emptiness, loneliness, feeling unloved and unlovable—an entire laundry list of unmet needs she had endured.
Finally, after allowing this for a sufficient length of time, the therapist got up, walked around the desk, and after asking the wife to stand, he embraced and kissed her long and passionately as her husband watched—with a raised eyebrow. The woman shut up and quietly sat down as though in a daze.
The therapist turned to the husband and said, "This is what your wife needs at least three times a week. Can you do this?"
"Well, I can drop her off here on Mondays and Wednesdays, but on Fridays, I fish."

A truck loaded with thousands of copies of *Roget's Thesaurus* crashed yesterday and lost its entire load. Witnesses were stunned, startled, aghast, taken aback, stupefied, confused, shocked, rattled, paralyzed, dazed, bewildered, mixed up, surprised, awed, dumbfounded, nonplussed, flabbergasted, astounded, amazed, confounded, astonished, overwhelmed, horrified, numbed, speechless, and perplexed.

What would you do if you saw someone having a seizure in a bathtub—throw your dirty laundry in? All jokes aside, though, you might want to be careful telling this joke. I was at a party last week and I told it to a guy there, and he didn't even crack a smile. In fact, he got pretty angry. He told me that his little brother had epilepsy and had died from having a seizure in a bathtub.

Obviously, I was mortified, so I said, "I'm so sorry. I had no idea. What happened? Did he drown?"

He turned to me, laughing, and screamed, "No, you idiot, he choked on a sock!"

Sam goes to mass and listens to the priest. After a while, the priest says that anyone who needs a special prayer should come up to the altar for a special blessing. Sam gets in line, and when it's his turn, the priest asks, "Sam, what do you want me to pray about for you?"

Sam replies, "Father, I need you to pray for my hearing."

The priest puts one finger in Sam's ear, places the other hand on top of Sam's head, and prays and prays and prays. After a few minutes, the priest removes his hands, stands back, and asks Sam, "How is your hearing now?"

Sam says, "I don't know, Father. It's not until next Wednesday!"

Last week, I opened my car door in a parking lot, accidentally dinging the car next to me. The driver jumped out of his car to yell at me. I couldn't help noticing that he was a dwarf as he flipped me off and screamed, "I am not happy!" Taking all this in, I answered, "Then which one are you?"

The nice, loving mother-in-law comes home and finds Eli, her son-in-law, furious and packing his suitcase.

"What happened?" she asks.

Eli screams, "What happened? I'll tell you what happened! I sent an email to my wife saying that I was coming home from my trip today. I got home, and guess what I found? My wife—yes, my Rachel, your daughter—with a guy in our marital bed! This is the end of our marriage. I will leave forever!"

"Calm down!" says the mother-in-law. "There's something odd about this story. Rachel would never do such a thing! Wait a minute while I check what happened."

Moments later, the mother-in-law comes back with a big smile. "You see, I said that there must be a simple explanation. Rachel never received your email."

An old marine pilot sat down at a coffee shop, still wearing his old USMC flight suit and leather jacket, and ordered a cup of coffee. As he sat sipping his coffee, a young woman sat down next to him. She turned to the pilot and asked, "Are you really a pilot?"

He replied, "Well, I've spent my whole life flying planes, first Stearmans, then the early Grummans ... flew a Wildcat and Corsair in WWII, and later, in the Korean conflict, Banshees and Cougars. I've taught more than 260 people to fly and given rides to hundreds, so I guess I am a pilot. And you, what are you?"

She said, "I'm a lesbian. I spend my whole day thinking about naked women. As soon as I get up in the morning, I think about naked women. When I shower, I think about naked women. When I watch TV, I think about naked women. It seems everything makes me think of naked women."

The two sat sipping in silence.

A little while later, a young man sat down on the other side of the old pilot and asked, "Are you really a pilot?"

He replied, "I always thought I was, but I just discovered I'm a lesbian."

On his seventy-fourth birthday, a man received a gift certificate from his wife. The certificate paid for a visit to a medicine man living on a nearby reservation who was rumored to have a wonderful cure for erectile dysfunction. After being persuaded, he drove to the reservation, handed his gift certificate to the medicine man, and wondered what he was in for.

The old man handed a potion to him and, with a grip on his shoulder, warned, "This is a powerful medicine. You take only a teaspoonful, and then say, "One, two, three.' When you do, you will become more manly than you have ever been in your life, and you can perform as long as you want."

The man was encouraged. As he walked away, he turned and asked, "How do I stop the medicine from working?"

"Your partner must say, 'One, two, three, four,'" he responded, "but when she does, the medicine will not work again until the next year."

He was very eager to see if it worked, so he went home, showered, shaved, took a spoonful of the medicine, and then invited his wife to join him in the bedroom. When she came in, he took off his clothes and said, "One, two, three!"

Immediately, he was the manliest of men. His wife was excited and began throwing off her clothes, and then she asked, "What was the one, two, three for?"

A woman is walking her toddler down on the beach. Suddenly, a huge wave comes up and sweeps her boy out to sea. The woman falls on her knees, lifts her head to the sky, puts her hands together, and says, "Please, *mien Gott*! If there is a heaven above, bring *mein* boy back to me!"

The clouds part. A huge wave emerges, and on the crest, coming in, is her boy. He swirls up to his momma. She looks down at him with tearful eyes, looks toward the heavens, and after a pause, says, "He had a cap."

During a church service, the pastor asked if anyone in the congregation would like to express praise for answered prayers. Suzie stood and walked to the podium. She said, "Two months ago, my husband, Phil, had a terrible bicycle accident and his scrotum was crushed."

There was a muffled gasp from the men in the congregation. "Phil was unable to hold me or the children," she went on, "and every move caused him terrible pain. We prayed as the doctors performed a delicate operation, and they were able to reconstruct the crushed remnants of Phil's scrotum, using wire to reinforce and shape it."

The men in the congregation cringed and squirmed uncomfortably.

"Now," she announced in a quivering voice, "thank the Lord, Phil is out of the hospital, and the doctors say that with time, his scrotum should recover completely."

All the men sighed with relief. The pastor rose and asked if anyone else had something to say. A man stood up and walked slowly to the podium. He said, "I'm Phil."

The entire congregation held its breath.

"I just want to tell my wife the word is *sternum*."

A woman is having an affair during the day while her husband is at work. Her nine-year-old son comes home unexpectedly, sees them, and hides in the bedroom closet to watch. The woman's husband also comes home. She puts her lover in the closet, not realizing that the little boy is in there already.

The little boy says, "Dark in here."

The man says, "Yes, it is."

Boy: "I have a baseball."

Man: "That's nice."
Boy: "Want to buy it?"
Man: "No, thanks."
Boy: "My dad's outside."
Man: "Okay, how much?"
Boy: "Two hundred fifty dollars."
In the next few weeks, it happens again that the boy and the lover are in the closet together.
Boy: "Dark in here."
Man: "Yes, it is."
Boy: "I have a baseball glove."
The lover, remembering the last time, asks the boy, "How much?"
Boy: "Seven hundred and fifty dollars."
Man: "Fine."
A few days later, the father says to the boy, "Grab your glove; let's go outside and have a game of catch."
The boy says, "I can't. I sold my baseball and my glove."
The father asks, "How much did you sell them for?"
Boy: "A thousand dollars."
The father says, "That's terrible to overcharge your friends like that. That is way more than those two things cost. I'm going to take you to church so you can confess your sins."
They go to the church and the father makes the little boy kneel in the confessional booth to wait for the priest. When the priest slides open the partition to hear the boy's confession, the boy says, "Dark in here."
The priest says, "Don't start that shit again."

Three friends married women from different parts of the country. The first man married a woman from Wisconsin. He told her that she was to do the dishes and house cleaning. It took a couple of days, but on the third day, he came home to see a clean house and dishes washed and put away.

The second man married a woman from Minnesota. He gave his wife orders that she was to do all the cleaning, dishes, and the cooking. The first day, he didn't see any results, but the next day, he saw it was better. By the third day, he saw his house was clean, the dishes were done, and there was a huge dinner on the table.

The third man married a girl from Tennessee. He ordered her to keep the house cleaned, dishes washed, lawn mowed, laundry washed, and hot meals on the table for every meal. He said the first day he didn't see anything, the second day he didn't see anything, but by the third day, some of the swelling had gone down and he could see a little out of his left eye.

One evening, a husband, thinking he was being funny, said to his wife, "Perhaps we should start washing your clothes in SlimFast. Maybe it would take a few inches off your butt!"

His wife was not amused and decided that she simply couldn't let such a comment go unnoticed. The next morning, the husband took a pair of his underwear out of his drawer.

"What the heck is this?" he said to himself as a little dust cloud appeared when he shook them out. "Sally!" he hollered into the bathroom. "Why did you put baby powder in my underwear?"

She replied with a giggle, "It's not baby powder; it's Miracle-Gro."

I would like to share a personal experience with all of you about drinking and driving. As you well know, some of us have been known to have had brushes with the authorities on our way home from an occasional social session over the years.

A couple of nights ago, I was out for an evening with friends and had a few cocktails and some rather nice red wine. Knowing full well that I may have been slightly over the limit, I did something I've never done before—I took a cab home. Sure enough, on the way there, I passed a police roadblock, but since it was a cab, they waved it past.

I arrived home safely without incident, which was a real surprise, as I have never driven a cab before and am not sure where I got it or what to do with it now that it's in my garage.

A married couple no sooner gets in bed when the husband passes gas and says, "Seven points."

His wife rolls over and says, "What in the world was that?"

The husband replies, "It's fart football."

A few minutes later, his wife lets one go and says, "Touchdown, tie score."

After about five minutes, the husband lets another one go and says, "Aha. I'm ahead 14–7."

Not to be outdone, the wife rips out another one and says, "Touchdown, tie score."

Five seconds go by, and she lets out a little squeaker and says, "Field goal, I lead 17–14."

Now the pressure is on for the husband. He refuses to get beaten by a woman, so he strains really hard. Since defeat is totally unacceptable, he gives it everything he's got and accidentally poops in the bed.

The wife says, "What the hell was that?"

The husband says, "Halftime, switch sides."

A woman wakes during the night to find that her husband is not in bed. She puts on her robe and goes downstairs to look for him. She finds him sitting at the kitchen table with a hot cup of coffee in front of him. He appears to be in deep thought, just staring at the wall. She watches as he wipes a tear from his eye and takes a sip of his coffee.

"What's the matter, dear?" she whispers as she steps into the room. "Why are you down here at this time of night?"

The husband looks up from his coffee. "It's the twentieth anniversary of the day we met."

She can't believe he has remembered and starts to tear up.

The husband continues. "Do you remember twenty years ago when we started dating? I was eighteen, and you were only sixteen," he says solemnly.

Once again, the wife is touched to tears.

"Yes, I do," she replies. The husband pauses; the words are not coming easily.

"Do you remember when your father caught us in the back seat of my car?"

"Yes, I remember," says the wife, lowering herself into the chair beside him. The husband continues.

"Do you remember when he shoved the shotgun in my face and said, 'Either you marry my daughter or I will send you to prison for twenty years'?"

"I remember that too," she replied softly.

He wiped another tear from his cheek and said, "I would have been a free man today."

Exercise for people over sixty: Begin by standing on a comfortable surface, where you have plenty of room on each side. With a five-pound potato bag in each hand, extend your arms straight out from your sides and hold them there as long as you can. Try to reach a full minute, and then relax. Each day, you'll find that you can hold this position a little longer.

After a couple of weeks, move up to ten-pound potato bags. Then try fifty-pound potato bags, and eventually try to get to the point where you can lift hundred-pound potato bags in each hand and hold your arms straight out for a full minute. (I'm at this level.) After you feel confident at that level, put a potato in each bag.

After nearly fifty years of marriage, a couple was lying in bed one evening, when the wife felt her husband begin to massage her in ways he hadn't in quite some time. It almost tickled as his fingers started at her neck and then began moving down past the small of her back. He then caressed her shoulders and neck, slowly worked his hand down, and stopped just over her stomach.

He then proceeded to place his hand on her left inner arm, working down her side, passing gently over her buttock and down her leg to her calf. Then he proceeded up her thigh, stopping just at the uppermost portion of her leg. He continued in the same manner on her right side, then suddenly stopped, rolled over, and became silent.

As she had become quite aroused by this caressing, she asked in a loving voice, "Honey, that was wonderful. Why did you stop?"

To which he responded, "I found the remote."

Jack, a handsome man, walked into a sports bar around 9:58 p.m. He sat down next to a blonde at the bar and stared up at the TV as the ten o'clock news came on. The news crew was covering a story of a man on a ledge of a large building preparing to jump. The blonde looked at Jack and said, "Do you think he'll jump?"

Jack said, "You know what? I bet he will."

The blonde replied, "Well, I bet he won't."

Jack placed thirty dollars on the bar and said, "You're on!"

Just as the blonde placed her money on the bar, the guy did a swan dive off the building, falling to his death. The blonde was very upset and handed her thirty dollars to Jack and said, "Fair's fair. Here's your money."

Jack replied, "I can't take your money, I saw this earlier on the five o'clock news and knew he would jump."

The blonde replied, "I did too, but I didn't think he'd do it again."

One morning, a husband returns to the cabin after several hours of fishing and decides to take a nap. Although not familiar with the lake, the wife decides to take the fishing boat out, since it is such a beautiful day. She motors out a short distance, anchors, and reads her book. Along comes the game warden in his boat. He pulls up alongside the woman and says, "Good morning, ma'am; what are you doing?"

"Reading a book," she replies (thinking, *Isn't that obvious?*).

"You're in a restricted fishing area," he informs her.

"I'm sorry, officer, but I'm not fishing. I'm reading."

"Yes, but you have all the equipment. I'll have to write you a ticket."

"For reading a book?" she replies.

"You're in a restricted fishing area," he informs her again.

"But, officer, I'm not fishing; I'm reading."

"Yes, but you have all the equipment. For all I know, you could start fishing at any moment. I'll have to write you a ticket, and you'll have to pay the fine."

"If you do that, I'll have to charge you with sexual assault," says the woman.

"But I haven't even touched you," says the game warden.

"That's true, but you have all the equipment. For all I know, you could start at any moment."
"Have a nice day, ma'am." He quickly departs.

A filthy-rich Florida man decided that he wanted to throw a party and invited all of his buddies and neighbors. He also invited Leroy, the only redneck in the neighborhood. He held the party around the pool in the backyard of his mansion. Leroy was having a good time drinking, dancing, eating shrimp, oysters and BBQ, and flirting with all the women.

At the height of the party, the host said, "I have a ten-foot man-eating gator in my pool and I'll give a million dollars to anyone who has the nerve to jump in."

The words were barely out of his mouth when there was a loud splash. Everyone turned around and saw Leroy in the pool. Leroy was fighting the gator and kicking its rear! He was jabbing it in the eyes with his thumbs, throwing punches, head butts and choke holds, biting the gator on the tail, and flipping it through the air like some kind of Judo instructor. Water was churning and splashing everywhere. Both Leroy and the gator were screaming and raising heck. Finally, Leroy strangled the gator and let it float to the top like a dime-store goldfish. Leroy then slowly climbed out of the pool. Everybody just stared at him in disbelief.

Finally, the host said, "Well, Leroy, I reckon I owe you a million dollars."

"No, that's okay. I don't want it," said Leroy.

The rich man said, "Man, I have to give you something. You won the bet. How about half a million bucks then?"

"No thanks. I don't want it," answered Leroy.

The host said, "Come on. I insist on giving you something. That was amazing. How about a new Porsche and a Rolex and some stock options?"

Again, Leroy said no. Confused, the rich man asked, "Well, Leroy, then what do you want?"

Leroy said, "I want the name of the sumbich who pushed me in the pool!"

A priest and a nun are caught in a blizzard. They find a deserted cabin and take shelter. They find a sleeping bag, a bed, and a pile of blankets. The priest, being a gentleman, offers the nun the bed and takes the sleeping bag for himself. As they get tucked in for the night, the nun calls out, "Father, Father, I'm cold!"

So the priest gets up and puts another blanket on the nun. "Is that better, Sister?" he asks.

"Yes, Father, much better," she replies.

He gets back in his sleeping bag and starts to nod off when she again calls out, "Father, I'm still cold!"

So once again, the priest gets up and puts another blanket on her, ensuring she is tucked into the bed well. "Is that better, Sister?" he asks.

"Oh, yes, Father; that's much better," she says.

So the priest gets himself back into the sleeping bag and this time is just starting to dream when he wakes up to her call of, "Father, Father, I'm just so cold!"

The priest thinks long about this and finally says, "Sister, we are in the middle of nowhere in a blizzard. No one but you, myself, and the Lord himself will ever know what happens here this night. How about, just for this night, we act as though we were married?"

The nun thinks on this for a minute. She can't help but admit to herself that she's been curious, and she finally answers with a tentative, "Okay, Father, just for tonight, we will act as though we are married."

So the father replies, "Get up and get your own damned blanket!" and rolls over to fall asleep.

A woman was at her hairdresser getting her hair styled for a trip to Rome with her husband. She mentioned the trip to her hairdresser, who responded, "Rome? Why would anyone want to go there? It's crowded and dirty. You're crazy to go to Rome. So, how are you getting there?"

"We're taking United," was the reply. "We got a great rate!"

"United?" exclaimed the hairdresser. "That's a terrible airline. Their planes are old, their flight attendants are ugly, and they're always late. So, where are you staying in Rome?"

"We'll be at this exclusive little place over on Rome's Tiber River called Taste."

"Don't go any further. I know that place. Everybody thinks it's gonna be something special and exclusive, but it's really a dump."

"We're going to go to see the Vatican and maybe get to see the pope." "That's rich." The hairdresser laughed. "You and a million other people trying to see him. He'll look the size of an ant. Boy, good luck on this lousy trip of yours. You're going to need it."

A month later, the woman again came in for a hairdo. The hairdresser asked her about her trip to Rome.

"It was wonderful," explained the woman. "Not only were we on time in one of United's brand-new planes, but it was overbooked, and they bumped us up to first class. The food and wine were wonderful, and we had a handsome twenty-eight-year-old steward who waited on us hand and foot. And the Taste Hotel was great! They just finished a $5 million remodel, and now it's a jewel, the finest hotel in the city. They, too, were overbooked, so they apologized and gave us their presidential suite at no extra charge!"

"Well," muttered the hairdresser, "that's all well and good, but I know you didn't get to see the pope."

"Actually, we were quite lucky, because as we toured the Vatican, a Swiss guard tapped me on the shoulder and explained that the pope likes to meet some of the visitors and that if I'd be so kind as to step into his private room and wait, the pope would personally greet us. Sure enough, five minutes later, the pope walked through the door and shook my hand! I knelt down, and he spoke a few words to me."

"Oh, really! What'd he say?"

He said, "Who screwed up your hair?

Four million of these people enter our country every year. They are uneducated, unskilled, and contribute nothing. They are a burden to honest, hardworking Americans, and

THOUGHTS ON THE POT | 129

our government is doing nothing to stop them—not to mention they're dirty and they smell bad. *They don't even speak English!* I'm not prejudiced; I just really hate babies.

A male whale and a female whale were swimming off the coast of Japan when they noticed a whaling ship. The male whale recognized it as the same ship that had harpooned his father many years earlier. He said to the female whale, "Let's both swim under the ship and blow out of our air holes at the same time, and it should cause the ship to turn over and sink."

They tried it, and sure enough, the ship turned over and quickly sank. Soon, however, the whales realized the sailors had jumped overboard and were swimming to the safety of shore. The male was enraged that they were going to get away and told the female, "Let's swim after them and gobble them up before they reach the shore."

At this point, he realized the female was becoming reluctant to follow him.

"Look," she said, "I went along with the blow job, but I absolutely refuse to swallow the seamen."

While taking his daily walk, a man finds a dirty, old whiskey bottle. In order to see the label, he gives it a rub. *Poof,* a genie pops out.

"I will grant you one wish and one wish only. The only catch is, you have only ten seconds to make your wish," says the genie.

The man looks down at the whiskey bottle and sees it fitting to make the following wish: "I wish to be able to piss out whiskey for the rest of my life."

"Your wish has been granted." The genie vanishes.

The man decides to test it out to see if it really came true. He unzips his pants and starts taking a piss. Low and behold, whiskey! Unable to contain his excitement, he rushes home and goes straight to his wife.

"Honey, you'll never guess what happened." He continues to tell his wife about his encounter. With his wife being obviously skeptical, he decides to prove it.

"Hand me those two glasses," says the man. He proceeds to unzip his pants and piss into the two glasses. His wife can barely contain her excitement as they sip on the greatest whiskey they've ever had. The next night, the wife brings two glasses, the man unzips again, and again, the couple indulge in a glass of fine whiskey. On the next night, the man asks his wife if she'd like a glass of whiskey.

"Of course," says the wife.

The man gets up and heads over to the kitchen but comes back to his wife with only one glass. He unzips his pants, pisses in it, and starts sipping. Confused, the wife asks where her glass is.

The man then says, "Honey, tonight, you get to drink from the bottle."

I picked up a hitchhiker, seemed like a nice guy. A few miles down the road, he asked me if I was afraid that he might be a serial killer. I told him the odds of two serial killers being in the same car were highly unlikely.

A car full of Irish nuns is sitting at a traffic light in downtown Dublin when a bunch of rowdy drunks pull up alongside of them.

"Hey, show us yer tits, ya bloody penguins!" shouts one of the drunks.

Quite shocked, Mother Superior turns to Sister Mary Immaculata and says, "I don't think they know who we are; show them your cross."

Sister Mary Immaculata rolls down her window and shouts, "Piss off, ya fookin' little wankers, before I come over there and rip yer balls off!"

Sister Mary Immaculata then rolls up her window, looks back at Mother Superior quite innocently, and asks, "Did that sound cross enough?"

A man joins the navy and is shipped out immediately to an aircraft carrier in the middle of the Pacific Ocean. The captain is showing the new recruit around the ship, when the recruit asks the captain what the sailors do to satisfy their urges when they're at sea for so long.

"Let me show you," says the captain. He takes the recruit down to the rear of the ship, where there's a solitary barrel with a hole in it.

"This'll be the best sex you'll ever have. Go ahead and try it, and I'll give you some privacy."

The recruit doesn't quite believe it, but he decides to try it anyway. After he finishes up, the captain returns.

"Wow! That was the best sex I've ever had! I want to do it every day!" "Fine. You can do it every day except for Thursday."

"Why not Thursday?"

"That's your day in the barrel."

A girl goes into the doctor's office for a checkup. As she takes off her blouse, the doctor notices a red *H* on her chest.

"How did you get that mark on your chest?" asks the doctor.

"Oh, my boyfriend went to Harvard, and he's so proud of it that he never takes off his Harvard sweatshirt, even when we make love," she replies.

A couple days later, another girl comes in for a checkup. As she takes off her blouse, he notices a blue *Y* on her chest.

"How did you get that mark on your chest?" asks the doctor.

"Oh, my boyfriend went to Yale, and he's so proud of it that he never takes off his Yale sweatshirt, even when we make love," she replies.

A couple days later, another girl comes in for a checkup. As she takes off her blouse, he notices a green *M* on her chest.

"Do you have a boyfriend at Michigan?" asks the doctor.

"No, but I have a girlfriend at Wisconsin; why do you ask?"

A wife goes on a business trip. When she returns, she finds a pair of panties in her dresser drawer that do not belong

to her. Furious, she questions her husband. The husband says, "I have no idea where they came from. I don't do the laundry!"
So the wife goes to the maid and questions her.
Indignant, the maid replies, "Madam, how should I know? These panties don't belong to me. I don't even wear panties; just ask your husband!"

Last Saturday night, I was at a bar enjoying a libation or two, when in walked my ex. After we exchanged pleasantries, I told her that when I'm making love to my new girlfriend, I always think about her.
She said, "You still miss me that much?"
I said, "No, I think about you to keep me from coming too soon."

A guy is getting a checkup from his doctor.
The doctor says, "Mr. Smith, it looks like you have residue from a suppository in your ear!"
Mr. Smith asks if he can call someone, and the doctor gives him permission.
"Hello, Margaret? Good news! I think I know where my hearing aid is."

Two old men are sitting on the front porch, just watching life pass by. Suddenly, a Great Dane walks across their front lawn. The dog stops, lies down, and begins licking itself.

The first old man says, "Boy, I sure wish I could do that."
The second old man says, "I don't know about that, but if I were you, I'd try petting him first."

A loser is having a hard time picking up women, so his well-traveled friend takes him to a nightclub in Nashville, where he guarantees him that he will score.
The loser enters the bar, sees a beautiful girl sitting alone at the bar, and begins to barrage her with pickup lines that he acquired from his friend. The young lady continues to ignore him but finally gives in.
She says, "Okay, I'll spend the night with you, but I've got to let you know up front that I'm on my menstrual cycle."
The loser looks at her and says, "No problem. I'll follow you on my moped."

A nun gets into a cab and tells the driver her destination. As they're going along, the driver says, "Sister, I confess that I've always had the fantasy of being kissed by a nun."
The nun says, "I will kiss you if you promise that you're single and Catholic."
"I'm both of those things," replies the driver.
"All right then," says the nun. "Pull into this dark alley."
When they stop, the nun gives him the deepest, longest, wettest French kiss ever. They resume the journey, and the driver says, "I'm feeling guilty, Sister. I lied. I'm married and Jewish."

"That's all right," says the nun. "My name is Kevin, and I'm on my way to a Halloween party!"

Santa comes down a chimney one Christmas Eve and, to his surprise, finds a gorgeous brunette waiting for him, wearing the sexiest lingerie imaginable.

"Santa," she purrs, "can you stay for a while?"

Santa says, "Ho, ho, ho! I've gotta go! Have to deliver toys to children, you know!"

She comes close, starts playing with his beard, and whispers in his ear, "Santa, don't you have a gift you would like to give me?"

Santa says, "Ho, ho, ho! I've gotta go! Have to spread Christmas cheer, you know!"

The brunette loosens her lingerie straps, giving Santa a view of her breasts, and says, "Santa, are you sure there's no gift you'd like to give me?"

Santa says, "Hey, hey, hey, might as well stay. Can't get up the chimney this way!"

Jane and Arlene are outside their nursing home, having a drink and a smoke, when it starts to rain. Jane pulls out a condom, cuts off the end, puts it over her cigarette, and continues smoking.

Arlene: "What in the hell is that?"

Jane: "A condom. This way, my cigarette doesn't get wet."

Arlene: "Where did you get it?"

Jane: "You can get them at any pharmacy."

The next day, Arlene hobbles herself into the local pharmacy and announces to the pharmacist that she wants a box of condoms.

The pharmacist, obviously embarrassed, looks at her kind of strangely (she is, after all, over ninety years of age) but very delicately asks what size, texture, and brand of condom she prefers.

"Doesn't matter, Sonny, as long as it fits on a Camel."

The pharmacist faints.

Larry finally found the nerve to tell his fiancée that he had to break off their engagement so he could marry another woman.

"Can she cook like I do?" the distraught woman asked between sobs.

"Not on her best day," he replied.

"Can she buy you expensive gifts like I do?"

"Nope, she's broke."

"Well, then, is it sex?"

"Nobody does it better than you, babe."

"Then what's the one thing she can do that I can't?"

"Sue me for child support."

I grew up going to parochial schools and received a solid Christian Catholic education, but that has almost nothing to do with this story. There was a girl in my class who kept falling asleep. This went on for three days. On the first day, the nun prodded her with a pencil and asked her, "Who created Adam and Eve?"

The girl woke up from the pain and shouted, "Good God!"

The nun said, "Correct."

On the next day, the girl fell asleep again. The nun once again poked her with her pencil and asked her, "Who gave Adam and Eve the ability to reproduce?"

The girl woke up and said, "Good God!"

The nun once again said, "Correct."

On the third day, the girl fell asleep again. The nun prodded her as hard as she could with her pencil and asked her, "What did Eve say to Adam when they had too many children?"

The girl, unaware of the question, woke up from the pain and yelled at the nun, "If you stick that thing in me one more time, I'll break it in half!"

A man was taking a cab to the airport when he realized he left his passport at home and had to go back to get it. He reached through the partition and gently tapped the driver on his shoulder to get his attention. The driver screamed and lost control of the cab, jumped a curb, nearly hit a tree and several pedestrians, and finally came to a stop inches away from a building.

For a moment, the cab was silent until the passenger spoke up. "I'm sorry. I had no idea such a gentle tap would startle you so!"

"Oh, no," replied the cabbie, "it's all my fault. This is my first day driving a cab. For the past thirty years, I drove a hearse."

Harvard Law professor: "Who will tell me how the law constitutes fraud?"

Student: "If you don't let me pass this class, you've committed fraud."

Law professor (shocked): "Oh, really? How so?"

Student: "According to the law, those who take advantage of another person's ignorance, causing them to sustain losses, has committed fraud and should be prosecuted to the full extent of the law."

Professor: "Young man, I believe you will make a fine attorney."

The chief poet of the town dies, so they have to elect a new one. The voting whittles the candidates down to two. The town holds a feast to choose the winner. The mayor stands up and declares that the winner shall be decided by voting on the poem the candidates can come up with on the spot, based on a subject of his choosing. The mayor announces the subject will be Timbuktu.

The first candidate stands up, thinks for a moment, and recites:

"It came across a stormy gale
Broad of beam and wide of sail

Its keel was white, its hull was blue
Its destination: Timbuktu"

The crowd erupts; they're cheering for the first candidate. The mayor calms the crowd, chiding them to remember they still must hear the other candidate's poem. The second candidate stands up, considers the crowd with utter solemnity, and says:

"A-hiking Tim and I went,
When we came upon three girls in a tent.
Since they were three and we but two,
I bucked one and Tim bucked two."

An elderly couple in a restaurant are sharing a meal—a single hamburger with fries. The wife carefully cuts the burger in half, and the husband begins to eat as she lovingly watches. A young couple sees this, walks over, and says, "Please allow us to buy your wife her own meal."
The gentleman answers, "Thank you, but we share everything."
They watch for a while, and the wife still hasn't taken a single bite. The couple, thinking, *That woman's making sure her husband is full before she eats her half,* approaches the table once more and says, "Really. It would be our pleasure to buy you your own meal."

She replies, "It's really quite all right. We do share everything."

The couple asks, "Then pardon us for asking, but why haven't you eaten yet?"

To which the wife replies, "Because I'm waiting for the teeth."

A man goes to his girlfriend's parents' house for Thanksgiving. He's really nervous, as this is his first time meeting her family and he's not sure what to expect. In fact, he's so nervous that it's giving him gas.

While they're sitting there watching TV in the family room, it isn't so bad, because the football game is on and it's kind of loud. Also, the parents' big old dog, Harold, is licking his balls, and everyone can hear that. So he can sit there and fart into the couch without anyone hearing a thing.

But then everybody gets called into the dining room and he still has really bad gas, though he relaxes a little when the dog moves under the table to continue licking his balls. After a while, he just can't hold it in anymore, and to his horror, the fart comes out with enough force to rattle the silverware. Nobody says anything for a moment before the mom yells, "Harold! Get out of there."

The dog slowly comes out from under the table and goes back to the living room. The guy is amazed, as everybody goes back to eating and talking; they think the dog did it. A little while later, he feels another fart coming, bigger than the first. He looks around and realizes the dog is back under the table licking its balls again. So he relaxes and lets

the gas go. This one shakes the table so hard, some of the silverware falls off. Everyone is quiet. Then the mom again yells, "Harold, get out of there!"
The dog obediently goes back to the living room. Twenty minutes pass and they are about to start dessert when he feels the mother of all farts trying to punch its way through his colon. He's really stressed, but a quick glance confirms the dog is back under the table! Feeling confident, he just lets it free. It shakes the silverware. It shakes the table. It shakes the windows. And suddenly, everything is quiet.
Until the mom yells, "Dammit, Harold. Get out from under the table right now before he craps on you!"

Another "meet the family" joke? Sure.

A boy is invited to Thanksgiving dinner at his girlfriend's parents' house so that they can meet him. They've been together a long time but haven't had sex yet. His girlfriend tells him that after he meets her parents, they can "get intimate." So, in preparation, he decides to get some condoms at the local drugstore. As this will be his first time, he doesn't know anything about condoms, so he tells the pharmacist his predicament and that he needs some guidance on what to buy. The pharmacist explains all about the differences between the brands, and after a long chat, the boy decides on a large box of "ribbed for her pleasure."

The time comes for the Thanksgiving dinner, and the young couple are seated at the dinner table across from the girl's parents. The girl is surprised to see the boy has his head bowed down, apparently deep in prayer.

She whispers to him, "I didn't know you were so religious!"

He whispers back, "I didn't know your father was a pharmacist!"

One day at the end of class, little Billy's teacher asked the class to go home and think of a story and then conclude with the moral of that story. The following day, the teacher asked for the first volunteer to tell their story.

Little Suzy raised her hand. "My dad owns a farm, and every Sunday, we load the chicken eggs on the truck and drive into town to sell them at the market. Well, one Sunday, we hit a big bump and all the eggs flew out of the basket and onto the road."

The teacher asked for the moral of the story. Suzy replied, "Don't keep all your eggs in one basket."

Next was little Bobby. "Well, my dad owns a farm too, and every weekend, we take the chicken eggs and put them in the incubator. Last weekend, only eight of the twelve eggs hatched."

Teacher asked for the moral of the story. Bobby replied, "Don't count your eggs before they're hatched."

Last was little Billy. "My uncle Ted fought in the Vietnam War. His plane was shot down over enemy territory. He jumped out before it crashed with only a case of beer, a machine gun, and a machete. On the way down, he drank the case of beer. Unfortunately, he landed right in the middle of a hundred Vietnamese soldiers. He shot seventy with his machine gun but then ran out of bullets, so he pulled out his machete and killed twenty more. The blade on his machete broke, so he killed the last ten with his bare hands."

Teacher looked in shock at Billy and asked if there was possibly any moral to his story.

Billy replied, "Don't fuck with Uncle Ted when he's been drinking."

———

A man walks into a bar one night, goes up to the bar, and asks for a beer.

"Certainly, sir. That'll be one cent," says the bartender.

"One penny?" exclaims the guy.

"That's right," the barman replies.

So the guy glances over at the menu and asks, "Could I have a nice, juicy T-bone steak with a loaded baked potato and a Caesar salad?"

"Certainly, sir," replies the bartender, "but all that comes to real money."

"How much money?"

"Four cents," the barman says.

"Four cents? Where's the guy who owns this place?"

The barman replies, "Upstairs with my wife."

"What's he doing with your wife?"

The bartender smiles. "The same thing I'm doing to his business."

———

A couple was golfing one day on a very exclusive golf course, lined with multimillion-dollar homes. On the third tee, the husband said, "Honey, be very careful when you drive the ball. Don't knock out any windows; it will cost a fortune to fix."

The wife teed off and shanked it right through the window off the biggest house on the course. The husband cringed and said, "I told you to watch out for the houses. Let's go apologize and see how much this is going to cost."

They walked up, knocked on the door, and heard a voice say, "Come in."

They opened the door and saw glass all over the floor and broken bottle lying on its side in the foyer. A man sitting on the couch said, "Are you the people who broke that window?"

"Yes, sorry about that," the husband replied.

"No, actually, I want to thank you. I'm a genie that was trapped for a thousand years in that bottle. You released me. I'm allowed to grant three wishes. I'll give you each one wish and keep one for myself."

"Okay, great!" the husband said. "I want a million dollars a year for life."

"No problem; it's the least I could do. And you, what do you want?" the genie said, looking at the wife.

"I want a house in every country in the world," said the wife.

"Consider it done," the genie replied.

"And what is your wish, Genie?" the husband asked.

"Well, since I have been trapped in that bottle, I haven't had sex with a woman in a thousand years. My wish is to sleep with your wife."

The husband looked at the wife and said, "Well, we did get a lot of money and all those houses, honey. I guess I don't care." It was okay with the wife too.

The genie took the wife upstairs and ravished her for two hours. After it was over, the genie rolled over, looked at the wife, and asked, "How old are you and your husband?"

"He's thirty-five, and I'm thirty-three," she replied.

"Wow! Thirty-five and thirty-three, and you still believe in genies?"

A young woman was preparing for her wedding. She asked her mother to go out and buy a nice, long, black negligee and carefully place it in her suitcase so it would not wrinkle. Well, Mom forgot until the last minute. So she dashed out and could only find a short, pink nightie. She bought it and threw it into the suitcase.

After the wedding, the bride and groom entered their hotel room. The groom was a little self-conscious, so he asked his new bride to change in the bathroom and promise not to peek while he got ready for bed. While she was in the bathroom, she opened her suitcase and saw the negligee her mother had thrown in there. She exclaimed, "Oh, no! It's short, pink, and wrinkled!"

Right then, her husband screamed, "I told you not to peek!"

A general-store owner hires a young female clerk with a penchant for very short skirts. One day, a young man enters the store, glances at the clerk, and looks at the loaves of bread behind the counter.

"I'd like some raisin bread, please," the man says politely. The clerk nods and climbs up a ladder to reach the raisin bread, located on the very top shelf. The man, standing almost directly beneath her, is provided with an excellent view.

As the clerk retrieves the bread, a small group of male customers gather around the young man, looking in the same direction. Pretty soon, each person is asking for raisin bread, just to see the clerk climb up and down. After a few trips, the clerk is tired and irritated. She stops and fumes at the top of the ladder, glaring at the men standing below. She notices an elderly man standing among the throng.

"Is yours raisin too?" the clerk yells testily.

"No," croaks the feeble old man. "But it's startin' to twitch."

A man boards an airplane and takes his seat. As he settles in, he glances up and sees the most beautiful woman boarding the plane. He soon realizes she is heading straight toward his seat. A wave of nervous anticipation washes over him. Lo and behold, she takes the seat right beside his. Anxious to strike up a conversation, he blurts out, "So, where are you flying to today?"

She turns and smiles and says, "To the annual nymphomaniac convention in Chicago."

THOUGHTS ON THE POT | 147

He swallows hard and is instantly crazed with excitement. Here's the most gorgeous woman he has ever seen, sitting right next to him, and she's going to a meeting of nymphomaniacs. Struggling to maintain his outward cool, he calmly asks, "And what's your role at this convention?" She flips her hair back, turns to him, locks onto his eyes, and says, "Well, I try to debunk some of the popular myths about sexuality."

"Really," he says, swallowing hard. "And what myths are those?"

She explains. "Well, one popular myth is that African American men are the most well-endowed when, in fact, it is the Native American Indian who is most likely to possess this trait. Another popular myth is that Frenchmen are the best lovers, when actually, it is men of Jewish descent who romance women best, on average."

"Very interesting," the man responds.

Suddenly, the woman becomes very embarrassed and blushes.

"I'm sorry," she says. "I feel so awkward discussing this with you, and I don't even know your name."

The man extends his hand and replies, "Tonto. Tonto Goldstein."

A small guy goes into an elevator, looks up, and notices a huge dude standing next to him. The big dude looks down upon the small guy and says, "Seven feet tall, 350 pounds, twenty-inch penis, three-pound left testicle, three-pound right testicle, Turner Brown."

The small guy faints. The big dude picks up the small guy and brings him to, slapping his face and shaking him, and asks, "What's wrong with you?"
The small guy says, "Excuse me, but what did you say?"
The big dude looks down and says, "Seven feet tall, 350 pounds, twenty-inch penis, three-pound left testicle, three-pound right testicle, Turner Brown."
The small guy says, "Thank God! I thought you said, 'Turn around.'"

The pastor goes to the elderly couple and asks, "Were you able to abstain from sex for the two weeks?"
The old man replies, "No problem at all, Pastor."
"Congratulations! Welcome to the church!" says the pastor.
The pastor goes to the middle-aged couple and asks, "Well, were you able to abstain from sex for the two weeks?"
The man replies, "The first week was not too bad. The second week, I had to sleep on the couch for a couple of nights, but yes, we made it."
"Congratulations! Welcome to the church," says the pastor.
The pastor then goes to the newlywed couple and asks, "Well, were you able to abstain from sex for two weeks?"
"Well, Pastor, we were not able to go without sex for the two weeks," the young man replies.
"What happened?" inquires the pastor.
The man says, "My wife was reaching for a can of corn on the top shelf and dropped it. When she bent over to pick it up, I was overcome with lust and took advantage of her right there."

"You understand, of course, this means you will not be welcome in our church," states the pastor.
"That's okay," says the young man. "We're not welcome at Kroger anymore either."

You know how jerks you don't like and that you would never do business with insist on giving you their business cards? I collect them and toss them in the glove compartment. Then, whenever I bump into a car or give them a little ding while opening my car door, I pull out one of those business cards, write "I'm sorry" on the back, and place it under their windshield wiper.

A boy went to his grandfather's house for a week. On the first night at dinner, he found a thick, slimy goo on his plate, so he said to his grandfather, "Grandpa, is this plate clean?"
"As clean as cold water can get it," his grandfather answered.
The next morning, the boy found sticky, dried goo on his fork, so he asked his grandfather, "Grandpa, is this fork clean?"
"As clean as cold water can get it," his grandfather said.
This went on for the rest of the week. On the last day when the boy was leaving, the dog was blocking the door, so he said, "Grandpa, your dog won't let me through."
His grandfather said to the dog, "Coldwater, go lie down."

A woman is in a coma and doctors fear it may be permanent. One day, when a nurse is giving her a sponge bath, she notices a response on the monitor when she's washing the patient's groin. The doctor explains to the husband what happened, telling him, "Crazy as this may sound, some medical literature indicates that maybe a little oral sex will do the trick and bring her out of her coma."

The husband is skeptical, but they assure him that they'll close the curtains for privacy. It's worth a try. The hubby finally agrees and goes into his wife's room. After a few minutes, the woman's monitor flatlines; she has no pulse and no heart rate. The doctor and nurses run into the room to attempt to resuscitate the woman.

"What happened?" the doctor asks.

The husband says, "I think she choked."

A girl was talking to her mother about her concern about her new boyfriend, who had been in an accident.

"He's sweet, he has a great job, and he takes great care of me," the girl said, "but I'm just not sure I can stay with him."

"So, what's wrong with him?" her mother asked.

"Well, he only has one foot," the girl said.

Her mother sighed into the phone and said, "Dear, that's nothing to worry about. Your father only has five inches."

Every day, a male coworker walks up very close to a lady at the coffee machine, inhales a big breath of air, and tells her that her hair smells terrific. After a week of this, she

THOUGHTS ON THE POT | 151

can't stand it anymore, and she takes her complaint to the supervisor in the HR department and asks to file a sexual harassment grievance against him.

The HR supervisor is puzzled and asks, "What's threatening about a coworker telling you your hair smells terrific?"

"It's Ralph," explains the woman.

"Ralph, the midget?" the supervisor asks.

A guy orders spaghetti in a restaurant. In the middle of eating, he finds a hair in his food. He says to the waiter, "I'm not paying for this dirty meal," and walks out.

The waiter watches the guy leave, walk across the street, and go into a whorehouse. The waiter waits about ten minutes, bursts through the door, and finds the guy with his face buried in pussy.

The waiter says, "You complain about one hair in your spaghetti, and you come over here and eat that?"

The man replies, "Yeah, and if I find any spaghetti in this pussy, I'm not paying for it either."

Two married buddies are out drinking one night when one turns to the other and says, "You know, I don't know what else to do. Whenever I go home after we've been out drinking, I turn the headlights off before I get to the driveway. I shut off the engine and coast into the garage. I take my shoes off before I go into the house. I sneak up the stairs, and I get undressed in the bathroom. I ease into bed, and my wife still wakes up and yells at me for staying out so late!"

His buddy looks at him and says, "Well, you're obviously taking the wrong approach. I screech into the driveway, slam the door, storm up the steps, throw my shoes into the closet, jump into bed, rub my hands on my wife's ass, and say, 'How about a blow job?' And she's always sound asleep."

One day, Harry came upon a big, long ladder that stretched into the clouds. He'd walked this way every day, and this ladder had never been there before. Curious and feeling brave, he began to climb. Eventually, he climbed into the layer of clouds and saw a rather large, homely woman lying there on a cloud. She said, "Take me now or climb the ladder to success!"

Harry figured success had to be better than that, so he continued climbing. He came upon another level of clouds and found a thinner, cuter woman than the one before. She said to him, "Take me now or climb the ladder to success!"

Harry saw that his luck was changing and so continued his climb. On another level of clouds, he found a rather attractive woman with not so bad of a figure. She said, "Take me now or climb the ladder to success!"

Harry really liked his chances now. He climbed quickly and deftly, and sure enough, on the next level, he found a gorgeous, lithe, well-endowed woman lying seductively on the cloud. "Take me now or climb the ladder to success," she whispered seductively.

Harry couldn't believe his eyes, but his greed got the best of him. He climbed to the next level, expecting to find a supermodel. Suddenly, the ladder ended, and a latch closed behind him. He looked over to see a four hundred-pound, seven-foot-tall, hairy, biker-looking guy with tattoos. The biker got up and walked menacingly toward Harry. Apprehensively, Harry whispered, "Who are you?"
The biker answered, "I am Cess!"

A woman arrives home from work, and her husband notices she's wearing a diamond necklace. He asks his wife, "Where did you get that necklace?"
She replies, "I won it in a raffle at work. Go get my bath ready while I start dinner."
The next day, the woman arrives home from work wearing a diamond bracelet. Her husband asks, "Where did you get that bracelet?"
She replies, "I won it in a raffle at work. Go get my bath ready while I start dinner."
The next day, her husband notices she arrives home from work wearing a mink coat. He says, "I suppose you won that in a raffle at work."
She replies, "Yeah, I did! How did you guess? Go get my bath ready while I start dinner."
Later, after dinner, she goes to take her bath, and she notices there is only one inch of water in the tub. She yells at her husband, "Hey! There's only an inch of water in the tub."
He replies, "I didn't want you to get your raffle ticket wet."

An adorable little girl walks into a pet shop and asks in the sweetest little lisp, "Excuse me, mithter, do you keep widdle wabbits?"

As the shopkeeper's heart melts, he gets down on his knees, so that he's on her level, and asks, "Do you want a widdle white wabbie or a thoft fuwwy black wabbie, or maybe a cute whittle bwown wabbie like the one over there?"

She blushes, rocks on her heels, puts her hands on her knees, leans forward, and says in a quiet voice, "I don't fink my pet python weally gives a thit."

Three babies in the womb discuss what they would like to be when they grow up. The first one says, "I want to be a plumber, so I can fix the pipes in here."

The second one says, "I want to be an electrician, so I can have some light in here."

The third one says, "I want to be a boxer."

The others look confused and ask, "Why do you want to be a boxer?"

He angrily replies, "So I can beat the hell out of that rude bald guy who keeps coming in here and spitting on us!"

A man tells his friend at a bar about the new girl he just met. "I've been chatting with her online. She's only sixteen years old, but she's so mature for her age! She's funny, sexy, and so flirty."

"Wow," says his friend, "it's surprising to meet a girl that young who is so mature."

"Yeah." The man nods. "And now she tells me she's an undercover cop. How cool is that at her age?"

A man on a business trip to Las Vegas heard that the Las Vegas prostitutes were amazing. On his first night there, he decided he would go out and try his luck. He walked outside his hotel and looked up and down the street and saw an attractive girl standing on the corner. He approached her and asked if she was working and, sure enough, she said, "Sure, let's go to my room."

He was in luck. She was a knockout. They got to the room, and he sat down anxiously on the edge of the bed. She asked him what he wanted and he thought for a second and then said how much for a hand job?

She said, "Three hundred."

His eyes popped open and he asked, "Three hundred dollars? For a hand job?"

She said, "Walk over to that window and open the curtains. See that motel down there? I own it, and I didn't inherit it. I'm that good."

He said, "Well, okay, go right ahead, honey."

So she proceeded to give him the best hand job he'd ever had. After a little rest, he asked, "How much for a blow job?"

She said, "Six hundred."

"Six hundred dollars? Oh my God," he replied.

She told him to walk back over to the window. "See that fifteen-story hotel? I own it, and I didn't inherit it. I'm that good."

He said, "Well, get to work then, sweetie."

And sure enough, he got the best blow job he had ever had. After a little recovery time, he asked, "How much for sex?" She chuckled and said, "Honey, if I had a pussy, I'd own this whole damned town."

A man named Bubba went hunting near the border of Alabama and Georgia. When he was heading back to his truck, a game warden came up to him and asked him what he had in the sack. Bubba said, "Three rabbits."

The warden said, "Let me see one of those rabbits."

So Bubba pulled out one of the rabbits. The warden stuck his finger in the rabbit's butt, pulled it out, smelled it, and said, "This is a Georgia rabbit. Let me see your Georgia hunting license."

Bubba showed him. Then the warden said, "Let me see another one of those rabbits."

So Bubba pulled out another rabbit. Then the warden stuck his finger in that rabbit's butt, tasted it, and said, "This is an Alabama rabbit. Let me see your Alabama hunting license."

Bubba showed it to him.

Then the game warden said, "Where are you from, boy?"

Bubba turned around, pulled his pants down, and said, "You tell me."

A man went to the doctor's office to get a prescription for a double dose of Viagra. The doctor told him that he couldn't allow him a double dose. "Why not?" asked the man.

"Because it's not safe," replied the doctor.
"But I need it really badly," said the man.
"Well, why do you need it so badly?" asked the doctor.
The man said, "My girlfriend is coming into town on Friday, my ex-wife will be here on Saturday, and my wife is coming home on Sunday. Can't you see? I must have a double dose."
The doctor finally relented and said, "Okay, I'll give it to you, but you have to come in on Monday morning so that I can check to see if there are any bad side effects."
On Monday, the man dragged himself in with his arm in a sling. The doctor asked, "What happened to you?"
The man said, "No one showed up."

A husband and wife have small children, so they decide to make a password for sex so they can speak in front of the kids. They decide on "washing machine." In bed one night, the husband says, "Washing machine!"
His wife replies, "Not tonight, darling. I have a headache."
Half an hour passes, and she feels really guilty, so she says, "Washing machine!"
Her husband replies, "Too late; it was only a small load, so I decided to do it by hand."

A father, mother, and son were going to Europe and were planning to visit the nude beaches while they were there. They didn't want the son to get a distorted view of beauty, so they told him the men with really big penises and the girls with really, really big boobs were both really, really dumb. When they got to the beach, they split up. Later, the mother saw the son and asked where his dad was.

The boy said, "Well, the last time I saw him, he was talking to this really, really, dumb blonde, and the longer they talked, the dumber he got."

A famous American golfer is invited to go to China for a golf tournament. From the second he gets there, he is treated like a king. He is given five-star treatment in a five-star hotel until the day of the tournament. The night before the tournament, he is sitting in his hotel room watching TV. A hot Chinese girl knocks on his door. He takes one look at her and says to himself, "Wow. They must really love me here."

He takes her to bed, but almost immediately, she yells, *"Chung hoi!"*

The golfer is pretty proud of himself, making a young girl scream like that. She continues to scream, *"Chung hoi! Chung hoi!"* all night long.

At the tournament the next day, the American golfer gets a hole in one and gets really excited. He starts yelling, *"Chung hoi! Chung hoi!"*

One of the Chinese golfers says, "What do you mean, 'wrong hole'?"

Benjamin asks his new girlfriend for a hand job.

"I've never done that," the naïve girl says. "What do I do?"

"Well," replies Benjamin, "remember when you were a kid and you'd shake a Coke bottle and spray your brother with it? That's what you do."

She nods, so he pulls his manhood out, and she grabs hold of it and starts shaking it. A minute later, he has tears running down his face, snot flowing from his nose, and wax flying from his ears.

She asks, "What's wrong?"

Benjamin cries, "Take your damn thumb off the end!"

A pastor entered his donkey in a race, and it won. The pastor was so pleased with the donkey that he entered it in the race again, and it won again. The local paper read: "Pastor's ass out front." The bishop was so upset with this kind of publicity that he ordered the pastor not to enter the donkey in another race.

The next day, the local paper headline read: "Bishop scratches pastor's ass." This was too much for the bishop, so he ordered the pastor to get rid of the donkey. The pastor decided to give it to a nun in a nearby convent.

The local paper, hearing of the news, posted the following headline the next day: "Nun has best ass in town." The bishop fainted. He informed the nun that she would have to get rid of the donkey, so she sold it to a farm for ten dollars. The next day, the paper read: "Nun sells ass for $10."

This was too much for the bishop, so he ordered the nun to buy back the donkey and lead it to the plains, where it

could run wild. The next day, the headlines read: "Nun announces her ass is wild and free."
The bishop was buried the next day.

In a terrible car accident, three nuns die at the same time. They all appear in front of the gates of heaven to meet Saint Peter. When they arrive, Peter informs them that those who lived a life of the cloth must answer some basic questions about theology before they are permitted to enter heaven. Each of the nuns has studied their Bible well, so they don't feel worried by this. The first nun steps forward and tells the saint that she's ready.
"Who was the first woman?" Peter asks.
"That's easy!" exclaims the nun. "Eve!"
Peter smiles, the bells toll, and the gates of heaven open up. The second nun, encouraged by her colleague's easy pass, steps forward and tells Peter that she's ready as well.
"Who was the first man?" Peter asks.
"Easy! That's Adam!" says the nun excitedly.
Peter smiles, the bells toll, and the gates of heaven open up. The third nun is now confident that she won't have any trouble, and she steps up to face Peter's question.
"What were Eve's first words to Adam?" he asks.
"My, that's a hard one," the nun replies worriedly, but Peter smiles, the bells toll, and the gates of heaven open up.

A couple driving home hit and wound a skunk on the road. The wife gets out and brings it back to the car. "We need to

THOUGHTS ON THE POT | **161**

take it to a vet. It's shivering; it must be cold. What should I do?" she asks.

Her husband replies, "Put it between your legs to keep it warm."

"But it stinks!" she exclaims.

"So, hold its damn nose!"

A teenage girl comes home from school and asks her mother, "Is it true what Rita just told me?"

"What's that?" asks her mother.

"That babies come out of the same place where boys put their penises?" said her daughter.

"Yes, it is, dear!" replied her mother, pleased that the subject had finally come up and that she wouldn't have to explain it to her daughter.

"But then, when I have a baby," responded the teenager, "won't it knock my teeth out?"

An Italian guy is out picking up chicks in Rome. While at his favorite bar, he manages to attract one rather attractive blonde tourist. He takes her back to his place, and sure enough, they go at it. After a long while, he climaxes loudly. Then he rolls over, lights up a cigarette, and asks her, "So, you finish?"

After a slight pause, she replies, "No."

Surprised, he puts out his cigarette, rolls back on top of her, and has his way with her again, this time lasting even longer than the first, and this time completing the deed with even louder shouts. Again, he rolls over, lights a cigarette, and asks, "So, you finish?"

And again, after a short pause, she simply says no. Stunned, but still acting reflexively on his macho pride, he once again puts out the cigarette and mounts his companion *du jour*. This time, with all the strength he can muster, he barely manages to end the task, but he does, after quite some time and energy is spent.

Barely able to roll over, he reaches for his cigarette, lights it again, and then asks tiredly, "So, you finish?"

Exhausted, she replies, "No, I'm Swedish."

Joe is on his last day at work as a mailman. He receives many thank-you cards and monetary gifts along his route. When he gets to the very last house, he's greeted by a gorgeous housewife who invites him in for lunch. Joe happily accepts. After lunch, the woman invites him up to the bedroom for some "dessert." Joe happily accepts again. When they are done, the woman hands Joe a dollar. Joe looks at her lying naked next to him and asks what the dollar is all about. The woman replies, "It was my husband's suggestion. When I told him that it was your last day at work, he told me, 'Screw him; give him a dollar.' The lunch was my idea."

While watching TV with his wife, a man tosses peanuts into the air and catches them in his mouth. Just as he throws another peanut into the air, the front door opens, causing him to turn his head. The peanut falls into his ear and gets stuck. His daughter comes in with her date. The man explains the situation, and the daughter's date says, "I can get the peanut out."

He tells the father to sit down, shoves two fingers into the father's nose, and tells him to blow hard. The father blows, and the peanut flies out of his ear. After the daughter takes her date to the kitchen for something to eat, the mother turns to the father and says, "Isn't he smart? I wonder what he plans to be."

The father says, "From the smell of his fingers, I'd say our son-in-law."

A guy is standing in a bar when a stranger walks in. After a while, they get to talking and drinking, and when he finally looks at his watch, he realizes it's 1:00 a.m.

"Oh, man, I'm screwed. I better get home. My wife has told me a thousand times not to stay out this late."

The other guy replies, "I'll help you out of this. Just do exactly what I say. Go home. Sneak into the bedroom. Pull back the covers. Get down between her legs and lick, lick, and lick for about twenty minutes, and there will be no complaints in the morning."

The guy agrees to try that and continues drinking with him for two more hours before heading home to give it a try. When he gets home, the house is pitch black. He sneaks upstairs into the bedroom, pulls back the covers, and proceeds to lick for twenty minutes. When he is finished, he decides to wash his face. As he walks into the bathroom, his wife is sitting on the toilet.

Seeing her, he screams, "What the hell are you doing in here?"

"Quiet!" she exclaims. "You'll wake up my mother."

Little Sally came home from school with a proud smile on her face. She told her mom, "Frankie Jones showed me his willy today."

Before her mom had a chance to respond, Sally said, "It reminded me of a peanut."

With a little smile, her mom asked, "Why? Was it really small?"

Sally replied, "No, really salty!"

"Doc, I think my son has a venereal disease," a patient told his urologist on the phone. "But the only woman he screwed is our maid."

"Okay, don't be hard on him. He's just a kid," the doctor soothed. "Get him in here right away, and I'll take care of him."

"But I've been screwing the maid too, and I've got the same symptoms he has."

"Then you come in with him, and I'll fix you both up," replied the doctor.

"Well," the man admitted, "I think my wife has it too."

"Oh, crap!" the physician roared. "That means we've all got it!"

Two old friends, one rich and one poor, are sitting at a bar having a few drinks. After a while, they realize that both of their wedding anniversaries are the next day. The poor man asks, "What did you get your wife for your wedding anniversary?"

The rich man replies, "I got her a red Ferrari and a diamond ring."

"Wow, what made you choose those gifts?"

The rich man says, "I wasn't sure about the ring, so if she doesn't like it, she can take it back in her new car."

The poor man nods in agreement. The rich man asks, "What did you get your wife?"

"I got her a pair of cheap slippers and a dildo."

The rich man asks, "Why did you choose those gifts?"

His poor friend responds, "Well, if she doesn't like the slippers, she can go fuck herself."

It once happened that a talented actor could no longer remember his lines. After searching for many years, trying to get his career back on track, he arrived at a theater that was willing to give him the chance to get back on the horse. The director cautioned him, "Take note that this is the most important part of the act, and you only have to say one line. You will perform it at the opening, and it will only require you to walk across the stage carrying a rose. Using only one finger and your thumb, hold the rose up to your nose, sniff on it deeply and say this line: 'Ahhh, my mistress's sweet aroma.'"

That's all he would have to do to make a comeback, so the actor was really excited. All day, as he waited for the play to begin in the evening, he rehearsed his career-saving line over and over again. Finally, the evening came. The curtain went up, the actor walked across the stage as he had been instructed to do, and he impeccably delivered the line: "Ahhh, my mistress's sweet aroma."

The theater exploded, the audience was dying of laughter, and the director was breathing fire. He cried, "You bloody fool! You have killed me! I'll never direct another play, thanks to you!"

Bewildered, the actor asked, "What did I do? Did I not say the line correctly?"

"No," the director screamed, "you idiot, you forgot the rose!"

Down at the club, John raised his beer and said, "Here's to living the rest of my life between my wife's legs."

The entire club applauded, and he won a prize for the best toast of the evening. He rushed home and excitedly told his wife, "Mary, I got a prize for the best toast of the night."

"What was the toast?" Mary inquired.

"I said, here's to living the rest of my life, sitting next to my wife at church," John lied.

"That is so good to hear," Mary replied.

The following day, while taking a stroll, Mary ran into one of John's drinking buddies. The man chuckled as he assured Mary that John had won the prize of the night courtesy of her.

Mary replied, "Yes, yes, I know all about that. It actually took me by surprise. You know, in the last four years, John has only gone there twice. One time, he dozed off, and the other, I was forced to drag him in there by the ears."

A very horny man is walking down the street wearing a black suit. He enters the first whorehouse he can find, and he is quickly kicked out for only offering five dollars. He enters the second and is kicked out again. By now, he is so horny that he feels like he is about to explode. He tries his luck at the next one, and with a weak voice, he says, "I am very horny. I've only got five dollars and could really use a blow job."

The attendant guy assuredly answers, "Worry not; with five dollars, we can offer you a penguin."

"What is a penguin?" the horny man asks.

"Wait and see!"

The attendant quickly takes the five dollars and ask the horny man to follow him into a bedroom. Happy to get something out of it, the man pulls down his black pants and lies on the bed, waiting. Soon enough, a beautiful prostitute walks into the room and starts giving the man the most amazing blow job of his life.

At the point where the man is about to explode, she stops and suddenly walks out of the room. Confused and with his black pants dragging around his ankles, the man waddles behind her, shouting, "What's a penguin? What's a penguin?"

Walking home after a girls' night out, two drunk women pass a graveyard and stop to pee. The first woman has nothing to wipe with, so she uses her underwear and tosses it. Her friend, however, finds a ribbon on a wreath, so she uses that.

The next day, the first woman's husband phones the second woman's husband, furious. "My wife came home last night without her panties!"

"That's nothing," says the other. "Mine came back with a card stuck between her butt cheeks that said, 'From all of us at the fire station. We will never forget you.'"

A young man and his date were parked on a back road quite some distance from town. They were about to have sex when the girl stopped him.

"I really should have mentioned this earlier, but I'm actually a hooker, and I charge $200 for sex."

The man reluctantly paid her, and they did their thing. After a cigarette, the man just sat there in the driver's seat, looking out the window.

"Why aren't we going anywhere?" asked the girl.

"Well, I should've mentioned this before, but I am actually a taxi driver, and the fare back to town is $250."

A man walks into a roadside diner and sees a sign hanging over the bar that reads: "Cheeseburger: $9.50. Chicken sandwich: $10.50. Hand job: $50."

The man walks up to the bar and beckons to one of the three exceptionally attractive blondes serving drinks.

"Can I help you?" she asks.

"I was wondering," whispers the man. "Are you the one who gives the hand jobs?"

"Yes," she purrs, "I sure am."

The man replies, "Well, go wash your hands. I want a cheeseburger."

A young man was showing off his new sports car to his girlfriend. She was thrilled at the speed and raw power and throaty exhaust.

"If I do two hundred miles per hour, will you take off your clothes?" he asked.

"Yes!" said his adventurous girlfriend.

And as he got up to two hundred mph, she peeled off all her clothes. He was unable to keep his eyes on the road, and the car skidded onto some gravel and flipped over. The naked girl was thrown clear of the car, but the boy was jammed beneath the steering wheel.

"Go and get help!" he cried.

"But I can't! I'm naked, and my clothes are gone!" she exclaimed.

"Take my shoe," he said, "and cover yourself!"

Holding the shoe in front of her, the girl ran down the road and found a service station. Still holding the shoe between her legs, she pleaded to the service station proprietor, "Please help me! My boyfriend is stuck!"

The proprietor looked at the shoe and said, "There's nothing I can do. He's in too far!"

One night, not too long ago, little Timmy sees his dad drinking bourbon. Little Timmy asks his dad, "Can I have some?"

His dad asks, "Can your dick touch your ass?"

Timmy replies no.

"Then no," his dad replies.

Later, he catches his dad looking at porn. Timmy asks, "Can I look at porn with you, Daddy?"

His dad asks again, "Can your dick touch your ass?"

"No," Timmy answers.

"Then no."

Later that night, little Timmy is eating cookies. His dad walks into the kitchen and asks, "Can I have a cookie?"

Timmy asks, "Can your dick touch your ass?"

His dad grins and replies, "Yes."

"Then go fuck yourself; these cookies are mine!"

Little Billy came home from school to see the family's pet rooster dead in the front yard. Rigor mortis had set in, and the bird was flat on his back with his legs in the air. When his dad came home, Billy said, "Dad, our rooster's dead, and his legs are sticking up in the air. Why are his legs sticking up in the air?"

THOUGHTS ON THE POT | 171

His father, thinking quickly, said, "Son, that's so God can reach down from the clouds and lift the rooster straight up to heaven."

"Gee, Dad, that's great," said little Billy.

A few days later, when his dad came home from work, Billy rushed out to meet him, yelling, "Dad, Dad, we almost lost Mom today!"

"What do you mean?" his father asked.

"Well, Dad, I got home from school early today and went up to your bedroom, and there was Mom, flat on her back with her legs in the air, screaming, 'Jesus, I'm coming; I'm coming!' If it hadn't been for Uncle George holding her down, we'd have lost her for sure!"

Little Johnny comes down to breakfast. Since they live on a farm, his mother asks if he has done his chores.

"Not yet," answers little Johnny. His mother tells him no breakfast until he does his chores. Well, he's a little pissed off, so he goes to feed the chickens, and he kicks a chicken. He goes to feed the cows, and he kicks a cow. He goes to feed the pigs, and he kicks a pig. He goes back in for breakfast, and his mother gives him a bowl of dry cereal.

"Why don't I get any eggs and bacon? Why don't I have any milk in my cereal?" he asks.

"Well," his mother says, "I saw you kick a chicken, so you don't get any eggs for a week. I saw you kick a pig, so you don't get any bacon for a week either. I also saw you kick a cow, so for a week, you aren't getting any milk."

Just then, his father comes down for breakfast and kicks the cat halfway across the kitchen. Little Johnny looks up at his mother with a smile and says, "Are you going to tell him, or should I?"

Paul was trying to find his way down a crowded street during a street fair when he suddenly spotted a palm reader. He stopped and went to sit at the gypsy's table.

"For just fifteen dollars, I will read your love line and predict your romantic future," the old, mysterious woman said. Paul was happy, and he readily agreed.

The lady took one look at his palm and said, "I can see that you do not have a girlfriend."

"That's true," Paul confirmed.

"Oh my, you are exceedingly lonely. Aren't you?"

"I am," Paul admitted shamefully. "You are so accurate. You can tell all of that from reading my love line?"

"Love line? No," said the gypsy," your calluses."

This young boy named Don walked into a whorehouse, slammed his money on the counter, and said, "I want a woman!"

The man behind the counter asked, "How old are you?"

Don replied, "I am seventeen!"

The man said, "You are too young; come back when you are older. Meanwhile, practice on trees."

"Trees?" Don asked.

"Yeah." The man nodded. "Go find yourself a nice hole in a tree."

A year later, Don once again came back to the whorehouse, swung the front door open, stomped over to the front desk, and slammed his money on the counter, harder than before. He screamed, "Give me a woman!"

The man behind the counter said, "How old are you?"

Don grinned. "I'm eighteen!"

The man took Don's money and said, "Okay, upstairs, second door on the left."

Don didn't miss a beat. He ran up those stairs so fast, he skipped every other step. About five minutes later, the man behind the counter heard the whore upstairs screaming in complete and utter agony. He jumped over the counter and ran up the stairs. Once at the room, he kicked in the door, and, to his surprise, Don had a broomstick shoved right into the poor girl.

The man shouted, "What the hell are you doing?"

Don replied simply, "Checking for squirrels."

A beautiful woman walks into a doctor's office, and the doctor is bowled over by how stunningly gorgeous she is. All his professionalism goes right out the window. He tells her to take her pants off; she does, and he starts rubbing her thighs.

"Do you know what I am doing?" asks the doctor.

"Yes, checking for abnormalities," she replies.

He tells her to take off her shirt and bra, and she takes them off. The doctor begins rubbing her breasts and asks, "Do you know what I am doing now?"

She replies, "Yes, checking for cancer."

Finally, he tells her to take off her panties, lays her on the table, climbs on top of her, and starts having sex with her. He says to her, "Do you know what I am doing now?"

She replies, "Yes, getting herpes; that's why I'm here!"

Jim decided to propose to Sandie, but before she could accept, Sandie confessed to Jim that she had suffered a childhood illness that left her breasts at the maturity of a twelve-year-old. Jim told her he loved her so much that it didn't matter to him at all, but that he had a confession of his own to make.

"I, too, have a problem. My penis is the same size as an infant, and I hope you can deal with that once we are married."

Sandie was a little disappointed, but she loved Jim, and he was so willing to overlook her flaw that she decided she had to overlook his.

Sandie said, "Yes, Jim, I will marry you and learn to live with your infant-sized penis."

Sandie and Jim got married, and as soon as they arrived in their hotel suite, they couldn't keep their hands off each other. As Sandie put her hand in Jim's pants, she suddenly screamed and ran out of the room. Jim ran after her to find out what was wrong.

She said, "You told me your penis was the size of an infant!"

"Yes, it is," Jim insisted. "It's eight pounds, seven ounces and nineteen inches long!"

A man escapes from prison, where he has been for fifteen years. He breaks into a house to look for money and guns and finds a young couple in bed. He orders the guy out of bed and ties him to a chair. While tying the girl to the bed, he gets on top of her, kisses her neck, and then gets up and goes into the bathroom.

While he's in there, the husband tells his wife, "Listen, this guy's an escaped convict; look at his clothes! He probably spent a lot of time in jail and hasn't seen a woman in years. I saw how he kissed your neck. If he wants sex, don't resist, and don't complain; do whatever he tells you. Satisfy him, no matter how much he nauseates you. This guy is probably very dangerous. If he gets angry, he'll kill us. Be strong, honey. I love you."

To which his wife responds, "He wasn't kissing my neck. He was whispering in my ear. He told me he was gay, thought you were cute, and asked me if we had any Vaseline. I told him it was in the bathroom. Be strong, honey. I love you too."

A few days after Christmas, a mother was working in the kitchen and listening to her young son playing with his new electric train in the living room. She heard the train stop, and her son said, "All you sons of bitches who want off, get the hell off now, because this is the last stop! And all you sons of bitches who are getting on, get your ass in the train, because we are heading down the tracks."

The mother went nuts and told her son, "We don't use that kind of language in this house. Now, I want you to go to your room, and you are to stay there for two hours. When you come out, you may play with your train, but I want you to use your nice language."

Two hours later, the son came out of the bedroom and resumed playing with his train. Soon, the train stopped, and the mother heard her son say, "All passengers who are disembarking from the train, please remember to take all your belongings with you. We thank you for riding with us today and hope your trip was a pleasant one. We hope you will ride with us again soon."

She hears the little boy continue, "For those of you just boarding, we ask you to stow all of your hand luggage under the seat. Remember, there is no smoking on the train. We hope you will have a pleasant and relaxing journey with us today."

As the mother began to smile, the child added, "For those of you who are pissed off about the two-hour delay, please see the bitch in the kitchen."

While vacationing with his wife in Las Vegas, a man went to see a show featuring one of the most famous magicians in the world. After an especially astounding act, the man, seated at the back with his wife, shouted, "How did you do that?"

"Sir, I could tell you, but I'd have to kill you after that," the magician replied.

The theater went silent for a couple of minutes before the man yelled back, "All right, then, come tell my wife!"

A bus full of nuns drives off a cliff, and sadly, they all die in a fiery crash. They arrive at the gates of heaven and meet Saint Peter. Saint Peter says to them, "Sisters, welcome to heaven. In a moment, I will let you all through the pearly gates, but first I must ask each of you a single question. Please form a single file line."

And they do so. Saint Peter turns to the first nun in the line and asks her, "Sister, have you ever touched a penis?"

The nun responds, "Well, there was this one time that I kinda, sorta touched one with the tip of my pinky finger."

Saint Peter says, "All right, Sister, now dip the tip of your pinky finger in the holy water, and you may be admitted," and she did so.

Saint Peter now turns to the second nun and says, "Sister, have you ever touched a penis?"

"Well, there was this one time that I held one for a moment."

"All right, Sister, now just wash your hands in the holy water, and you may be admitted," and she does so.

At this, there is a jostling in the back of the line as one nun is trying to cut in front of another. Saint Peter sees this and ask the nun, "Sister Susan, what's the matter? There's no rush!"

Sister Susan responds, "Well, if I'm going to have to gargle with it, I'd rather do it before Sister Mary sticks her butt in it!"

Harry and his wife are having hard financial times, so they decide that she will become a hooker. She is not quite sure what to do, so Harry says, "Just stand in front of that bar and pick up a guy. Tell him that you charge $200. If you have a question, I'll be parked around the corner."
She is standing there for a few minutes when a guy pulls up and asks, "How much?"
She says, "Two hundred bucks."
He says, "All I've got is fifty."
"Hold on," she says and runs back to Harry. She asks him, "What can I give for fifty dollars?"
"A hand job," Harry replies. She runs back and tells the guy all he gets for fifty bucks is a hand job. He agrees, and she gets in his car. He unzipped his pants, and out pops an enormous penis. She stares at it for a minute and then says, "I'll be right back."
She runs back to Harry's car and asks him, "Can you loan this guy $150?"

A guy walks into the local whorehouse and says, "I want the cheapest one you've got; I don't have much money."
The guy behind the counter says, "How about the $1.95 special?"
The customer says, "Great!"

He pays and happily heads to the room. When he opens the door, he finds a remarkably beautiful young girl lying on the bed, naked with her legs wide open, just waiting for him. He rips off his clothes and starts going to town on her. Suddenly, all this white stuff starts coming out of her mouth, nose, and even her ears. The man panics and jumps out of bed. He runs to the desk and tells the guy what happened. The guy just nods and then says to the janitor, "Hey, Joe, the dead one's full again."

Two cowboys are having a beer at a bar and talking about sex. The first cowboy says, "I like the rodeo position."
"Can't say I've heard of the rodeo position," the second cowboy says as he takes a sip of his beer. "What is it?"
"Well, you get a girl down on all fours and mount her from behind. Then you reach around and grab both of her breasts and whisper in her ear, 'These feel just like your sister's tits.' Then you try to hold on for eight seconds!"

Five friends were playing poker and planning their upcoming fishing trip. One of them, Steve, had to tell them that he couldn't go because his wife wouldn't let him. After a lot of teasing and name-calling, Steve headed home, frustrated. The following week, when Steve's buddies arrived at the lake to set up camp, they were shocked to see Steve. He was already sitting at the campground with a cold beer, fishing rod in hand and a campfire glowing.
"How did you talk to your wife into letting you go, Steve?"

"I didn't have to," Steve replied. "Yesterday, when I left work, I went home and slumped down in my chair with a beer to drown my sorrows because I couldn't go fishing. Then my wife snuck up behind me and covered my eyes and said, 'Surprise!' When I pulled her hands back, she was standing there in red lingerie. She said to me, 'Carry me into the bedroom, take me to the bed, and do whatever you want.' So I tied her to the bed and went fishing."

John is paying a visit to his Italian neighbor in the hospital, who just had a very serious traffic accident. He looks bad—all plaster, completely wrapped up in a bandage, tons of tubes in his veins; he looks like a mummy. John tries to have a conversation, but his neighbor has his eyes closed and isn't responding. Suddenly, his eyes jump wide open, and he starts to gargle, and during his last gasp for air, he says, *"Mi stai, bioccando il d'tubicino assigeno, pezzo di merda!"*

John inscribes these Italian words in his heart. At the funeral, John tells the black-clad widow that her husband had something to say.

"What was it?" she asked with tearful eyes, "Was it that he loved me?"

"I don't know," said the man, "but it sounded like, *'Mi stai, bioccando Il d'tubicino assigeno, pezzo di merda.'*"

The widow screams and faints. John turns, startled, to the daughter and asks, "What did he say? What does that mean?"

The crying daughter says, "It means, 'You're standing on my oxygen hose, you ass!'"

A baby was born that was so advanced that he could already talk. He looked around the delivery room and saw his mother. He looked at his mother and asked, "Are you my mother?"

"Yes, I am," she said.

"Thank you for taking such good care of me before I was born," he said.

He then looked at his father and asked, "Are you my father?"

"Yes, I am," his father answered.

The baby motioned for him to come closer. The father did, and the baby poked him on the forehead with his index finger five times and said, "I want you to know that really hurts!"

A married couple went to the hospital to have their baby delivered. When they arrived, the doctor said he had invented a new machine that would transfer a portion of the mother's pain to the baby's father. The doctor asked if they were willing to be part of this trial. The husband agreed, so the doctor set up the pain transfer. The wife's labor started to progress, so the doctor set the pain transfer to 10 percent, for starters, explaining that even 10 percent was probably more pain than the father had ever experienced.

However, as the labor progressed, the husband felt fine and asked the doctor to go ahead and kick it up a notch.

The doctor then adjusted the machine to 20 percent pain transfer. The husband was still feeling fine. The doctor checked the husband's blood pressure and was amazed by how well he was doing. The doctor asked the husband if he wanted to increase the pain transfer. Seeing that he was feeling well, he agreed.

The pain transfer was obviously helping the wife considerably, so the husband encouraged the doctor to transfer all the pain to him. And in no time, the wife delivered a healthy baby girl with nearly no pain! The couple was ecstatic, and the doctor was baffled at how well the trial had gone.

When the couple got home, they found the mailman dead on their front porch.

It is Gary's birthday. His wife decides to spice things up this year for his birthday, so she takes him to a strip club as his gift. They arrive at the club and the doorman says, "Gary! How are you?"

His wife is puzzled and asks Gary if he has ever been to this club before.

"Oh, no," says Gary. "He is on my bowling team."

When they are seated, a waitress tells Gary she will bring him his usual. Shortly after, a double Johnnie Walker on the rocks arrives. His wife is becoming increasingly uncomfortable and says, "How did she know that you drink Johnnie Walker on the rocks?"

"Oh, honey, she's in the ladies' bowling league. We share lanes with them."

A stripper named Candy Cane works her way over to the table. Candy throws her arms around Gary and says, "Hey, Gary! Want your usual lap dance, big boy?"

Gary's wife is now furious. She grabs her purse and storms out of the club. Gary follows her and spots her getting into a cab. Before she can slam the door, he jumps in beside her. He tries desperately to explain how the stripper must have mistaken him for someone else, but his wife is having none of it. She is screaming and calling him every name in the book.

The cab driver turns his head and says, "Looks like you picked up a real bitch tonight, Gary."

A guy is talking to his doctor about his physical results. The doctor says, "Everything checked out okay, but I gotta tell ya—you have the dirtiest balls I've ever seen."

The guy returns home, opens the door, and sees his wife vacuuming busily.

"Honey, I need to talk to you about my physical."

"Not now!" she says. "I'm so busy, I don't have time to wipe my own ass!"

He says, "That's what I need to talk to you about."

A couple was celebrating their thirtieth wedding anniversary. For the entire time they had been married, the wife had kept a safe, and the husband had never been allowed to look inside it.

He asked her, since they had been married so long, if he could see what she had been keeping all these years. She said okay and opened the safe. In it was a pile of money totaling $100,000 and three chicken eggs.

He asked her, "What are the eggs doing in there?"

She said, "Well, I have to admit that I haven't been completely faithful to you. Whenever I strayed, I put an egg in the safe."

He thought about it and said, "Well, I guess I can't be too upset about three eggs. But where did all the money come from?"

She replied, "Every time I got a dozen, I sold them."

A lady goes to the doctor and complains that her husband is losing interest in sex. The doctor gives her a pill but warns her that it's still experimental. He tells her to slip it into his mashed potatoes at dinner, so that night, she does just that. About a week later, she's back at the doctor, where she says, "Doc, the pill worked great! I put it in the potatoes like you said! It wasn't five minutes later that he jumped up, raked all the food and dishes onto the floor, grabbed me, ripped all my clothes off, and ravaged me right there on the table!"

The doctor says, "I'm sorry; we didn't realize the pill was that strong! The foundation will be glad to pay for any damages."

"Nah," she says, "that's okay. We're never going back to that restaurant anyway."

I was stuck in a bad traffic jam in Washington, DC. Some random guy came up to my car and knocked on the window. I rolled it down and asked him what was going on. He said, "Terrorists have kidnapped the entire US Congress. They want $100 million or they're going to douse them all with gasoline and set them on fire. We're going from car to car to collect donations."
So I asked, "On average, how much is everyone giving?"
The man replied, "About a gallon."

A daughter walks in and says, "Dad, why is my name Butterfly?"
The father replies, "Well, when you were born, a butterfly landed on your head."
Then the second daughter walks in and asks, "Dad, why is my name Lily?"
The dad replies, "Well, when you were born, a lily flew in from the window and landed softly on your head."
Then the son comes in and says, "Hdow dar do babby?"
The dad quickly says, "Shut up, Cinderblock!"

At school, little Johnny's classmate tells him that most adults are hiding at least one dark secret, so it's very easy to blackmail them by saying, "I know the whole truth."
Little Johnny decides to go home and try it out. Johnny's mother greets him at home, and he tells her, "I know the whole truth."

His mother quickly hands him twenty dollars and says, "Just don't tell your father."

Quite pleased, the boy waits for his father to get home from work and greets him with, "I know the whole truth."

The father promptly hands him forty dollars and says, "Please don't say a word to your mother."

Very pleased, little Johnny is on his way to school the next day when he sees the mailman at his front door. The boy greets him by saying, "I know the whole truth."

The mailman immediately drops the mail, opens his arms, and says, "Then come give your daddy a hug!"

At a Sunday family lunch, a daughter, a twenty-year-old excellent student, announces that she is pregnant. Father drops his fork and knife in shock. Mother looks at her in total disbelief. None of them are able to say a word for a couple of seconds, and then the yelling starts.

What was she thinking? Of course, she doesn't plan to keep it? They invested so much in her education; how could she do this? Who is the father?

"Don't worry," she says, "the father-to-be will be here in a couple of minutes to meet you."

Ten minutes later, a luxury sports car parks in the driveway. A very nice-looking young man in a custom-tailored Gucci suit gets out of the car and enters the house.

"Good afternoon, ma'am; sir," he says, introducing himself. As he shakes their hands, diamonds sparkle on his expensive watch. "We find ourselves in this situation, but we were not planning this," he continues. "However, a child would be more than welcome in our family. So let me lay the plan out for you. Should this child be a boy, God bless us, my father decided to let him run his bank, as soon as he finishes Harvard. I, however, plan to let him run my car-manufacturing company; it's not as big a deal as banking, but still, since they are luxury cars, the company has a couple of billion in revenue yearly.

"If the baby happens to be a girl, my mother insists that she get her education in Italy, so after she is ready, she can run her high-fashion business in Milan, where she would live in our villa on Lake Como. If, however, unfortunately, your daughter has a miscarriage—"

"Then, my son," the father interrupts him, putting his hand on the young man's shoulder, "you will bang her again."

A beautiful young woman was driving through a remote part of Texas when her car broke down. An American Indian on horseback soon came along and offered her a ride to the next town. She climbed up behind him on the horse, and they rode off. The ride was uneventful, except that every few minutes, the Indian would shout out a wild, "Ye-e-e-e-e-ha-a-a," so loud that it echoed off the surrounding hills.

When they arrived in town, he let her off at the local gas station. She expressed her thanks, and he yelled a final, "Ye-e-e-e-e-ha-a-a!" and rode off.

"Why was that Indian so excited?" asked the gas station attendant.

"I don't know. I just rode behind him on the horse with my arms around his waist and held onto the saddle horn so I wouldn't fall off," the woman answered.

"Lady," the attendant said, "Indians don't use saddles."

A woman places an ad in the local newspaper: "Looking for a man with three qualifications: won't beat me up, won't run away from me, and is great in bed."

Two days later, her doorbell rings. "Hi, I'm Tim. I have no arms, so I won't beat you, and no legs, so I won't run away."

"What makes you think you are great in bed?" the woman retorts.

Tim replies, "I rang the doorbell, didn't I?"

Getting my kids to behave at Christmas time was impossible. "He's making a list, checking it twice, gonna find out who's naughty or nice?" Nope. The Elf on a Shelf? Not even close. So one night when they had all gone to bed, I wrapped empty boxes and put them under the tree. Every time they acted up, I grabbed a "gift" and threw it in the fireplace. Problem solved.

Bobby had been married a long time, so he was devastated to come home from work and find a note saying Susie had left him.

"I don't know what I'm gonna do," he cried.

I said, "Let's be pragmatic and look at all of this logically."

"Okay," he whimpered. I asked him some questions.

"Now that she's gone, who's going to keep you awake with her snoring?"

Through his tears, he replied, "Nobody."

"And who's going to gripe about the way you drive?"

He sniffled and said, "Nobody."

"And who's going to bitch about your drinking, pot smoking, and gambling?"

Finally smiling, he replied, "Not nobody, not no how!" And with that, he stripped and ran down the street, screaming, "I'm free, finally *free!*"

And that's how you console a friend while stealing a line from *The Wizard of Oz*.

My buddy James is so annoying; he brags all the time. When his phone rings while we're hanging out, he shouts, "I'm blowing up, everybody!" like it's some kind of contest. Eventually, he went so far as to change his ring tone to him shouting, "I'm blowing up, everybody!"

Last week, he asked me to drop him off at the airport. When he got out of my car, I gave him just enough time to get to airport security, then I called him on his phone.

A man saw a lady with big breasts. He asked, "Excuse me; can I bite your breasts for $1,000?"

She agreed, so they went to a secluded corner. She opened her blouse, and the man fondled her breasts, motorboating and sucking on them for ten minutes.

Eventually, the lady asked, "Aren't you going to bite them?"
He replied, "No, that's way too expensive."

At the National Art Gallery in Dublin, a husband and wife were staring at a portrait that had them completely confused. The painting depicted three black men totally naked, sitting on a bench. Two of the figures had black penises, but the one in the middle had a pink penis. The curator of the gallery realized that they were having trouble interpreting the painting and offered his personal assessment. He went on for over half an hour, explaining how it depicted the sexual emasculation of African Americans in a predominately white patriarchal society.

After the curator left, an Irishman approached the couple and said, "Would ya like to know what the paintin' is really all about?"

"Now, why would you claim to be more of an expert than the curator of this gallery?" asked the couple.

"Because I'm the artist who painted it," he replied. "In fact, there are no African Americans depicted here at all. They're just three Irish coal miners. And the guy in the middle? Well, he's the one who went home for lunch."

My young daughter: "Dad, my boyfriend says I have a wonderful chassis, lovely airbags, and a beautiful bumper."
Me: "Tell your boyfriend that if he opens your hood and tries to check your oil with his dipstick, I'll tighten his nuts

so hard, his headlights will pop out and he'll start leaking from his tail pipe!"

A husband exclaims to his wife one day, "Your butt is getting really big. It's bigger than the BBQ grill!"
Later that night in bed, the husband makes some advances toward his wife, who completely shuts him down.
"What's wrong?" he asks.
She answers, "Do you really think I'm gonna fire up this big-assed grill for one little weenie?"

When I was single, I tried one of those internet dating sites. She was pretty, but she wasn't much of a conversationalist. She wouldn't kiss me. She didn't even want to cuddle. I think she was way more interested in my money than me. And that dating site was insanely expensive. I am so done with Ashley Madison.

A cowboy was taken prisoner by a bunch of angry Indians. They were all prepared to kill him, but their chief declared that since they were celebrating the Great Spirit, they would grant the cowboy three wishes before killing him. The cowboy could do nothing but obey them. The chief came up to him and asked, "What do you want for your first wish?"
"I want talk to my horse," replied the cowboy.

The chief allowed him to talk to the horse. The cowboy whispered in its ear. The horse neighed, reared back, and took off at full speed. About an hour later, the horse came back with a naked lady on its back. Well, the Indians were quite impressed, so they let the cowboy use one of their teepees. A little while later, the cowboy stumbled out of the teepee, tucking in his shirt.

The chief asked him once again, "What do you want for your second wish?"

"I want to talk to my horse again," replied the cowboy.

Once more, he whispered in the horse's ear. The horse neighed, reared back, and took off at full speed. About an hour later, the horse came back with another naked lady on its back. Well, the Indians were very impressed indeed. So, once again, they let the cowboy use one of their teepees. The cowboy stumbled out a little while later.

The chief came up to the cowboy and asked, "So, what do you want for your last wish?"

"I want to talk to my damn horse," replied the exhausted cowboy.

He grabbed the horse by the ears and yelled, "You stupid animal, I said *posse, posse*—not *pussy*!

Yesterday, scientists revealed that beer contains small traces of female hormones. To prove their theory, the scientists fed a hundred men twelve beers a day for a month. They observed that 100 percent of them gained weight, talked excessively without making sense, became emotional, couldn't drive, and refused to apologize when wrong. No further testing is planned.

At the party for our twenty-fifth wedding anniversary, I asked my wife, "Darling, have you ever been unfaithful to me?"

"Yes, honey, three times."

"When was the first time?"

"Do you remember when you went to the bank but nobody would give you any credit, and finally, the CEO of the bank himself signed the credit allowance for you?"

"Thanks, sweetie. And when was the second time?"

"Do you remember when you were extremely ill and nobody would agree to do the surgery for you, and finally, the head of the department took care of you?"

"Thank you, my love; you saved my life. And with whom were you unfaithful to me for the third time?"

"Do you remember when you were a candidate for mayor, and you were eighty-seven votes short?"

A man and a woman are having dinner in a restaurant. Their waitress, taking another order at a table a few paces away, spots that the man is slowly sliding down his chair and under the table, with the woman acting unconcerned. As the waitress watches, the man slides all the way under and out of sight. Still, the woman dining opposite him appears not to notice.

Finally, the waitress comes over to the table and whispers discreetly to the woman, "Pardon me, ma'am, but I think your husband just slid under the table."

"No, he didn't," the woman calmly replies. "He just walked in the door."

The conductor of an orchestra went crazy when one of his musicians played the wrong note. The conductor jumped down and stabbed him with his baton, killing him. He was given the death penalty. For his last meal, he wanted a dozen bananas. They hit the switch on the electric chair, and nothing happened. They explained that they had to let him go free.

He got his job back at the orchestra, and during the next performance, he killed another band member for screwing up. Back to prison and the electric chair. He again requested a dozen bananas for his last meal. When they hit the switch, like before, nothing happened. Before letting him go, they asked if it has something to do with the bananas.

"No, he replied, "I'm just a bad conductor." (*Groan*)

Golden Oldie: Two Italian guys get on a bus. They sit down and engage in an animated conversation. The lady sitting behind them ignores them at first, but her attention is galvanized when she hears one of the men say the following: "Emma come first. Den I come. Den two asses come together. I come once a more. Two asses, they come together again. I come again and pee twice. Then I come one lasta time."

"You foul-mouthed swine," retorted the lady indignantly. "In this country, we don't talk about our sex lives in public!" "Hey, coola down, lady," said the man. "Who talkin' abouta sexa? I'm a justa tellin' my frienda how to spella *Mississippi*."

Father O'Malley rose from his bed one morning. It was a fine spring day in his new west Texas mission parish. He walked to the window of his bedroom to get a deep breath of the beautiful day outside. He then noticed there was a jackass lying dead in the middle of his front lawn. He promptly called the local police station.

The conversation went like this:

"Good morning. This is Sergeant Jones. How can I help you?"

"And the best of the day te yerself. This is Father O'Malley at Saint Ann's Catholic Church. There's a jackass lying dead in me front lawn, and would ye be so kind as to send a couple o'yer lads to take care of the matter?"

Sergeant Jones, considering himself to be quite a wit and recognizing the foreign accent, thought he would have a little fun with the good father and replied, "Well, now, Father, it was always my impression that you people took care of the last rites!"

There was dead silence on the line for a long moment. Father O'Malley then replied, "Aye, 'tis certainly true, but we are also obliged to notify the next of kin first, which is the reason for me call."

When I was a young guy, I went on a date with an exceptionally beautiful woman. After a few drinks, I asked her, "Would you bang a guy for $50,000?"
She said, "Sure!"
So I asked, "Would you bang a guy for a hundred bucks?"
She said, "Hell no; what kind of a girl do you think I am?"
I said, "I already know what kind of girl you are. I'm haggling over the price."

Violent crimes have increased dramatically. Last night, I was imbibing at my favorite local saloon, when a woman I didn't even know came up to me and asked me to walk her to her car.
I thought about it, then I said, "I'd be happy to help you, but with both of us out there, wouldn't that potentially double the risk of a crime?"
She flipped me off. I went back to my cocktail.

Regina married and had thirteen children. When her husband died, she married again and had seven more children. Again, her husband died. So, Regina remarried and this time had five more children. Sadly, Regina herself finally passed away. Standing before her coffin, the priest prayed for her.
He thanked the Lord for this very loving woman and said, "Thank the Lord; they're finally together."
One mourner leaned over and quietly asked her friend, "Do you think he means her first, second, or third husband?"
The friend replied, "I think he means her legs."

A rabbi, a Hindu, and a lawyer are in a car. They run out of gas and are forced to stop at a farmer's house. The farmer says that there are only two extra beds, and one person will have to sleep in the barn.

The Hindu says, "I'm humble; I'll sleep in the barn," so he goes out to the barn.

In a few minutes, the farmer hears a knock on the door. It's the Hindu, and he says, "There is a cow in the barn. It's against my beliefs to sleep with a cow."

So the rabbi says, "I'm humble; I'll sleep in the barn."

A few minutes later, the farmer hears another knock on the door, and it's the rabbi. He says that it is against his beliefs to sleep where there is a pig, and there is a pig in the barn. So the lawyer is forced to sleep in the barn.

A few minutes later, there is a knock on the door. It's the pig and the cow.

My grandmother had a way with words and a wicked sense of humor. When the time came, she put my granddad in one of those assisted-living facilities. I called her to see how it was going.

She said, "Oh, Patrick, he took to it like a fish out of water!"

Startled, I asked, "Is that good?"

She said, "Good? It's great. He died last Tuesday!"

I bet the bartender $500 that if he placed fifteen shot glasses anywhere on the bar, I could balance on my unicycle, fill every glass with pee, and not spill a drop on his bar.

He laughed and took the bet. I got up there and peed everywhere. What a mess. The bartender laughed his butt off, shook my hand, grabbed my $500, and cleaned up all the pee.

Still laughing, he said, "You must be some kind of stupid to make a bet like that."

I said, "Not as dumb as I look. I bet your bouncer $1,000 that I could pee all over your bar and that you would laugh, shake my hand, and clean it up."

A mom is driving a little girl to her friend's house for a playdate. "Mommy," the little girl asks, "how old are you?"

"Honey, you are not supposed to ask a lady her age," the mother warns. "It is not polite."

"Okay," the little girl says, "how much do you weigh?"

"Now, really," the mother says, "these are personal questions and are really none of your business."

Undaunted, the little girl asks, "Why did you and daddy get a divorce?"

"Those are enough questions, honestly!" The exasperated mother walks away as the two friends begin to play.

"My mom wouldn't tell me anything," the little girl says to her friend. "Well," says the friend, "all you need to do is look at her driver's license. It's like a report card; it has everything on it."

Later that night, the little girl says to her mother, "I know how old you are; you are thirty-two."

The mother is surprised and asks, "How did you find that out?"

"I also know that you weigh 140 pounds."
The mother is past surprise and shock now. "How in heaven's name did you find that out?"
"And," the little girl says triumphantly, "I know why you and daddy got a divorce."
"Oh, really?" the mother asks. "Why?"
"Because you got an F in sex."

I walked into the post office last week to see a middle-aged, balding man standing at the counter methodically placing "Love" stamps on bright-pink envelopes with hearts all over them. He then took out a perfume bottle and started spraying scent all over the envelopes. My curiosity was piqued, so I went up to the balding man and asked him what he was doing.
The man said, "I'm sending out 1,000 Valentine cards signed, 'Guess who?'"
"But why?" I asked.
"I'm a divorce lawyer," the man replied.

A psychiatrist was showing me around the insane asylum and decided to show me a test they used to decide whether people should be admitted as patients.
"We fill a bathtub with water and we hand the person a teaspoon, a cup, and a pail and ask them how they would go about emptying it."
"Oh," I said, "so the normal person will use the pail to empty the tub." The doctor replied, "No, actually, a normal

person would pull the plug. So, would you like a private room?"

Billy went to see his doctor and nervously asked if he had ever laughed at a patient. The doctor reassured him, "In over twenty years, I haven't laughed at a single patient, because I always remain thoroughly professional."

With that, Billy dropped his pants, revealing the tiniest penis the doctor had ever seen. It wasn't any bigger than a AAA battery.

The doctor just couldn't help himself and burst into uncontrollable laughter before composing himself and saying, "I'm sorry; I really am. I don't know what came over me. I promise it won't happen again. Now, what seems to be the problem?"

Billy said, "It's swollen."

Johnny came home to find his wife with her suitcases packed in the living room.

"Where the hell do you think you're going?" Johnny asked.

"I'm going to Las Vegas. You can earn $400 for a blow job there, and I figured I might as well earn money for what I do to you for free."

Johnny thought about that for a moment, ran upstairs, and came back down with his suitcase packed as well.

"Where do you think you're going?" the wife asked.

"I'm coming with you. I want to see how you survive on $800 a year!"

After twenty years of marriage, I suggested to my wife that we should invent a little code for when she wants sex, so I don't have to read her mind at bedtime. That night, as we got into bed, I said, "So, if you want to have sex, pull my penis one time. If you don't want to have sex, pull my penis 256 times."

Roger got on the elevator at the AT&T building in downtown Nashville. He made small talk with an elderly woman and said, "Good mornin'."
She said, "Looks like rain."
He said, "Typical Nashville weather."
She slapped the crap out of Roger.
"Ow! What the hell? All I said was 'typical Nashville weather!'"
She said, "Oh, I'm so sorry. I thought you said, 'Tickle your ass with a feather!'"

I went into the confessional box after years of being away from the church. I discovered a fully equipped bar with several single-malt bottles of scotch and Guinness on tap. On the other wall was a dazzling array of the finest cigars and chocolates. Then the priest came in.
"Father, forgive me. It's been a long time since my last confession, but first, I must say that the confessional box is much more inviting than it used to be."
The priest replied, "Get out. You're on my side."

A woman and baby are at the doctor's office. The doctor is concerned about the baby's weight.
"Is he bottle fed or breastfed?"
The woman replies, "Breastfed."
The doctor gets her to strip down to her waist so he can examine her breasts. He pinches her nipples, rubs and sucks on them for a few minutes, then says, "Well, no wonder the baby is underweight; your breasts have no milk."
The woman replies, "I know. I'm his grandmother!"

When he was twelve, I caught my son watching porn on the internet. No, it was worse than that. His older sister caught him. Yeah, not good. So, I knew the time had come for me to have "the talk" with him. I was straight-up honest as I told him how everything worked. And that when it's over, the most important thing a guy must always remember to do—is to erase his search history.

My accountant was confused about a bill he had received, so he asked his secretary for some help with the math.
"If I were to give you $20,000, minus 14 percent, how much would you take off?" he asked her.
The secretary replied, "Everything but my earrings."

Life is unpredictable. You can chase your dreams wherever they lead and wind up lost, alone, and a long way from home. Or it can all work out and you find yourself rich,

THOUGHTS ON THE POT | **203**

successful, and dearly loved by all. Either way, dream big and buckle up, buttercup. It's gonna be one hell of a ride.

A woman was taking her late husband to the undertaker. He was wearing his best charcoal-gray suit. The woman knew it was her husband's dying wish to be buried in a blue suit, something that they had never been able to afford when he was alive. She told the undertaker of her husband's wish, acknowledging that she couldn't afford a new suit, and she asked him if there was anything he could do. The undertaker told the widow that he would do what he could and to come back in three days.

When the widow returned three days later, she found her husband in his coffin, wearing a stunning blue suit. She was overcome with gratitude and asked the undertaker how he'd managed this.

The undertaker replied, "Not half an hour after you left, a lady brought in her late husband, who was wearing a blue suit. She told me how he'd always wanted to be buried in a gray suit, but she couldn't afford a new one, so I told her I'd see what I could do and to return in three days. After she'd left, I checked, and he was about the same height and build as your husband, so I swapped the heads."

I guess you'd say I'm old fashioned. When we got engaged, I went to my fiancée's dad to discuss our plans with him. "Sir, I am asking for your daughter's hand."

He said jokingly, "Why? I don't get it. Don't you already have a hand?"

Laughing, I quipped, "I do, sir, but I'm sick and tired of my own hand!"

I have a small lake on my property. It's surrounded by fruit trees. Yesterday, I grabbed a bucket and headed down there to pick some apples. I was surprised to discover some young women skinny-dipping in the lake. When they noticed me, they swam to the deeper water.

One of them shouted, "We're not coming out until you leave!"

Raising my bucket, I shouted back, "Swim as much as you want. I just came down here to feed the alligators."

An Irishman went to confession in Saint Patrick's Catholic Church.

"Father," he confessed, "it has been one month since my last confession. I had sex with Fanny Green twice last month."

The priest told the sinner, "You are forgiven. Go out and say three Hail Marys."

Soon thereafter, another Irishman entered the confessional. "Father, it has been two months since my last confession. I've had sex with Fanny Green twice a week for the past two months."

This time, the priest questioned, "Who is this Fanny Green?"

"A new woman in the neighborhood," the sinner replied.

"Very well." The priest sighed. "Go and say ten Hail Marys."
At mass the next morning, as the priest prepared to deliver the sermon, a tall, voluptuous, drop-dead gorgeous redheaded woman entered the sanctuary. The eyes of every man in the church fell upon her as she slowly sashayed up the aisle and sat down right in front of the priest. Her dress was green and very short, and she wore matching, shiny emerald-green shoes. The priest and the altar boy gasped as the woman in the green dress and matching green shoes sat with her legs spread slightly apart, but just enough to realize she wasn't wearing any underwear.

The priest turned to the altar boy and whispered, "Is that Fanny Green?"

The bug-eyed altar boy couldn't believe his ears but managed to calmly reply, "No, Father, I think it's just a reflection from her shoes."

Jimmy, a nudist buddy of mine, gets engaged to a beautiful woman named Wendy. He loves her so much, he tattoos her name on his erect penis. When it's flaccid, the tattoo says *WY*. The couple decides to go to Jamaica on their honeymoon. Naturally, they choose a nudist resort. They have a wonderful time partying with their fellow nudists. Jimmy goes up to the bar to get a couple of rum drinks. He notices the bartender has *WY* tattooed on his penis.

Amazed, he says, "I see your *WY* there; by any chance, is your wife's name Wendy?"

The bartender says, "Oh, no, mon, I'm single. My tattoo says, 'Welcome to Jamaica; have a wonderful day!'"

One day, a woman feeling particularly lonely walked into a sex shop. The cashier asked if she needed help, to which she replied, "Yes, I would like the best dildo you have; price is not an issue."

The cashier asked her to wait a moment and disappeared into the back of the store. When he returned, he was holding a dusty and ancient-looking box. When he opened the box, inside was a normal-looking dildo.

"What's so special about this?" the woman asked.

The cashier explained that this was a *magic* dildo, and all you needed to do was say, "Magic dildo, _____" and fill in the blank with whatever you wanted the dildo to bang, and it would do exactly that.

The woman returned home with her new merchandise, eager to try it out. She went up to her room with the dildo and said, "Magic dildo, my vagina!"

The next hour was filled with the best sex she had ever had. Soon, she realized there was a problem. She couldn't get the magic dildo to stop! Panicked, she got into her car and raced over to the sex shop, hoping to catch the cashier before the store closed. Unfortunately, on the way over, she was pulled over by a cop.

"What's the big rush?" the policeman asked.

The woman, now in pain, proceeded to tell the police officer the story of her strange day, to which the cop scoffed, "Ha! Magic dildo, my ass!"

While we're on the subject: this old man and woman had been married for thirty years. In those thirty years, the woman had always insisted on the lights being off when they made love, as she was embarrassed. The man was actually thankful for this, as he was embarrassed too and scared that he couldn't please her, so in the dark, he always used a big dildo on her. After all these years of sex, she still had no idea that's what he did.

One night, she decided that they'd been together so long that there was no reason to be embarrassed, even though her body was now old. So, in the middle of sex, she reached over and turned the bedside lamp on, only to see that her husband was using a dildo.

She said angrily, "I knew it, asshole; explain the dildo!"

The man replied, "Okay, I will, but first—you explain the kids!"

Recently, I got home, plopped down in my recliner, and said, "Honey, get me a beer before it starts."

She grabbed me a cold one, and I downed it. Once again, I said, "Honey, get me a beer before it starts."

She grabbed one, and I downed it. I said, "Honey—"

She screamed, "You come in here ordering me around? Get up off your fat ass and get your own damned beer!"

So I said, "Too late, it already started."

One day, a nun and a stoner got on a bus. The stoner whispered in her ear, "You wanna have sex?"

She screamed, "Get away from me, you pervert!"

As the stoner got off the bus, he whispered to the driver, "Tell the nun to meet me in the cemetery at ten tonight." Sure enough, the nun showed up at ten to find the stoner disguised as Jesus. The stoner said, "I command you to have sex with me!"

The nun said, "Okay, but can you do it from behind?"

He did, and when he was finished, he yanked off his mask and said, "Ha, ha! I'm the stoner from the bus!"

That's when the nun stood up and said, "Ha, ha, ha! I'm the bus driver!"

When I lived in California, I had a pet parrot named Cracker. One day, Cracker swallowed a Viagra tablet. I was angry and disgusted, so I put him in the freezer to cool off. Later, when I opened the freezer, I found Cracker the parrot sweating.

"How come you are sweating?" I asked.

Cracker replied, "Do you have any idea how hard it is to pry open the legs of a frozen chicken?"

Back in college, I used to bartend on the weekends to make extra money. One night, a beautiful Irish girl came in who happened to be completely naked. She came up to the bar and said, "Gimme a pint of Guinness and a shot of Jameson."

I poured, never taking my eyes off her. When I served her, she asked, "Why are you staring at me? Haven't you ever seen a naked woman?"

I said, "Sure, lots of times. I'm just watching to see where you get the money to pay for these drinks."

Three women are discussing their teenage daughters. The first declares, "I was so shocked last week. I was tidying my daughter's room, and I found a pack of cigarettes under her pillow. I didn't know she smoked!"

"It gets worse than that," says the second mother. "I was tidying my daughter's room last week, and I found a bottle of vodka under her bed. I didn't know she drank!"

"Oh, it gets even worse than that," says the third mother. "I was tidying my daughter's room last week, and you'll never guess what I found in her bedside table: a pack of condoms! I didn't know she had a penis!"

It's 1962, and Bobby goes to pick up his date, Peggy Sue. Peggy Sue's father answers the door and invites him in. He asks Bobby what they're planning to do on the date. Bobby politely responds that they'll probably just go to the malt shop or to a drive-in movie.

Peggy Sue's father suggests, "Why don't you kids go out and screw? I hear all the kids are doing it."

Bobby is shocked. "Excuse me, sir?"

"Oh, yes, Peggy Sue really likes to screw. She'll screw all night if we let her."

Peggy Sue comes downstairs and announces that she's ready to go. About twenty minutes later, a thoroughly disheveled Peggy Sue rushes back into the house, slams the door behind her, and screams at her father, "Dad! It's The Twist! It's called The Twist!"

A psychiatrist is speaking to a large group of people who have had experiences with the paranormal.
"How many of you have seen a ghost?"
They all raise their hands.
"How many of you have touched a ghost?"
About half of them raise their hands.
"Okay, how many of you have made love to a ghost?"
One guy in the back row raises his hand. "Sir, do you mean to tell me that you've actually made love to a ghost?"
"Ghost? No, no, no, I thought you said *goat*!"

I live next door to a ninety-three-year-old man with dementia. Every morning at 8:00 a.m., he knocks on my front door to ask me if I've seen his wife. I have to tell him she's been dead for twenty years. I don't have to do this. I could pack up and move away, but I choose to stay, because nothing makes me happier than the smile on that old man's face.

Last New Year's Eve, my wife, Sally, stood up in our local pub and said that it was time to get ready. At the stroke of midnight, she wanted every husband to be standing next to the one person who made his life worth living. Well, it was kind of embarrassing. As the clock struck twelve, the bartender was almost crushed to death.

Two hunters are out in the woods. Suddenly, one of them keels over. The other hunter sees him lying there, not breathing. He pulls out his phone and dials *9-1-1*.
He screams, "Help! I think my friend just died, and I don't know what to do!"
The operator says in a calm, reassuring voice, "I can walk you through the procedure. The first thing we need to do is make sure he's dead."
There is a long silence, then a shot is heard. The hunter comes back on the phone.
"Okay, now what?"

On my eighteenth birthday, my dad sat me down for a little talk.
He said, "Son, I know you want to go out with your friends to celebrate being legal, but please heed my warning. Don't go to one of those vulgar strip clubs, because you will see things in there that you really shouldn't see."
So naturally, my friends and I headed straight for the nearest strip club.
Once inside, I realized he was absolutely right. There was a man stuffing singles into a hot stripper's g-string. So I walked right over to him, tapped him on the shoulder, and said, "Hi, Dad."

A proper lady was on an airplane in first class and was seated next to a man with a handkerchief in his lap. About half an hour after takeoff, the man sneezed. He calmly opened his fly, took out his penis, and wiped it with the handkerchief. The lady was shocked but a little too shy to say anything. About fifteen minutes later, he sneezed again and then once more opened his fly, grabbed his penis, and wiped it off. The lady could not believe it, and being too shy to mention it, she thought, *If he does that again, I'm definitely going to say something.*

About ten minutes later, the man sneezed again and proceeded as before.

She turned to him and said, "That is disgusting! Must you do that in front of me?"

He apologized and explained that it was a medical condition. "Every time I sneeze, I have an orgasm."

"Really? What do you take for that?" she asked.

The man replied, "Pepper."

Jimmy got blackout drunk at the annual Christmas party at work. He woke up with a crushing hangover, knowing he must have done something stupid. His wife poured him a coffee and told him in no uncertain terms, "You made a complete ass of yourself last night. You even cussed out your boss!"

Jimmy said, "Well, piss on him."

"You did, and he fired you!"

"Screw him!"

"I did; you go back to work on Monday."

A deaf guy goes to Walgreens to buy condoms and tries to explain what he wants with sign language. The pharmacist doesn't understand what he's trying to say, so the deaf guy pulls out his penis and fifty bucks. The pharmacist then pulls out his own penis, takes the fifty bucks, and puts the cash in his pocket.

The deaf guy goes completely insane and starts waving his arms in the air like a madman.

The pharmacist calmly says, "Chill out, dude. If you can't handle losing, you shouldn't make a bet."

This year at our family Thanksgiving dinner, my five-year-old niece, Sarah, was seated opposite me. I noticed she wasn't eating much, and she was staring at me. I thought, *Did I spill food on my shirt? No. Is something on my face? No.*

Everyone noticed her staring at me. Finally, her mom spoke up.

"Sarah, why are you staring at Uncle Pat?" Everyone got quiet.

She said, "Oh, I was just watching to see when Uncle Pat starts drinking like a fish!"

An old woman went to see her doctor.

She said, "Doc, I am tired of living. I'm ready to die. What's the best way to commit suicide?"

The doctor pondered this and said, "Well, if you must know, the quickest way to die would be to shoot yourself under your left breast."

She thanked him and went home. The next day, the old woman hobbled into the doctor's office.

Shocked to see her, he asked, "What happened?"

Disgusted, she replied, "I shot myself in the knee!"

A beautiful woman is sunbathing in the nude on the roof of a five-star hotel. A server from the restaurant comes up there and says, "Ma'am, the hotel manager would like you to put your clothes back on."

Indignant, she responds, "I most certainly will not! First, I am lying on my tummy; no one can see anything. Second, if someone comes up here, I have a huge beach towel to cover myself up—"

The server interrupts. "And third, you are sunbathing on the skylight above the restaurant."

I know it's wrong, but I don't have a fishing license. Wouldn't you know it, I got caught in the act by a game warden.

He said, "You're going to pay a hefty fine for all those fish in your bucket."

I said, "But, officer, I didn't catch these; these are my pet fish, and I just bring them here to swim. When they're done, they jump back into the bucket."

"Oh, really? This, I've got to see. If you can prove it, I'll let you go."

I emptied my bucket into the lake and waited patiently. A few minutes went by, and nothing happened.

The game warden asked, "So, where are the fish?"
I said, "What fish?"

A young lady walks into an upscale jewelry store. She browses around, spots a beautiful diamond bracelet, and walks over to inspect it. As she bends over to look more closely, she inadvertently breaks wind. Embarrassed, she looks around nervously to see if anyone has noticed her little toot and prays that a salesperson doesn't pop up right then.

As she turns around, her worst nightmare is realized in the form of a salesman standing right behind her. Cool as a cucumber and displaying complete professionalism, the salesman greets the lady with, "Good day, madam. How may we help you today?"

Very uncomfortably, but hoping that the salesman may not have been there at the time of her little "accident," she asks, "Sir, what is the price of this lovely bracelet?"

He answers, "Madam, if you farted just looking at it, you're going to shit when I tell you the price."

A psychiatrist was conducting a group therapy session with three young mothers and their small children.

"You all have obsessions," he observed. To the first mother, he said, "You are obsessed with eating. You even named your daughter Candy."

He turned to the second mom. "Your obsession is money. Again, it manifests itself in your child's name, Penny."

At this point, the third mother got up, took her little boy by the hand, and whispered, "Come on, Dick; let's get out of here."

Two girlfriends were catching up at the bar.
"Judy, my husband and I broke up."
"Kathy, that's horrible; why?"
"Well, do you think you could live with someone who smokes weed, drinks all day, is unemployed, and cusses like a sailor?"
"No, of course not!"
"Neither could he."

Smoking used to be everywhere—in restaurants, bars, airports, on planes, everywhere. Then they invented smoking sections. Now, smokers are relegated to glass cages at the airport. I like to look at 'em all in there, sucking their lives away. It's like a zoo for primates with a death wish.

I piled my luggage on the scale at the Southwest Airlines counter in Nashville and said to the ticket agent, "I'm flying to Los Angeles. I want the large bag sent to Denver and the two small ones sent to Cincinnati."
"I'm sorry, sir, but we can't do that," said the ticket agent.
"That's good to hear, because that's where they ended up the last time I flew with you."

A ninety-year-old man was having his annual checkup. The doctor asked how he was feeling.

"I've never been better!" he boasted. "I've got a twenty-two-year-old bride who's pregnant and having my child! What do you think about that?"

The doctor considered this for a moment, then said, "Let me tell you a story. I knew a guy who was an avid hunter. He never missed a season. But one day, he went out in a bit of a hurry and accidentally grabbed his umbrella instead of his gun. So he was in the woods, and suddenly, a grizzly bear appeared in front of him. He raised up his umbrella, pointed it at the bear, and squeezed the handle. And do you know what happened?" the doctor queried.

Dumbfounded, the old man replied, "No, what?"

The doctor continued, "The bear dropped dead right in front of him."

"That's impossible!" exclaimed the old man. "Somebody else must have shot that bear!"

"Exactly!" shouted the doctor.

Dear Dad,

It is with great regret and sorrow that I'm writing you. I had to elope with my new girlfriend, because I wanted to avoid a scene with Mom and you. I've been finding real passion with Stacy. She is so nice, but I knew you would not approve of her because of all her piercings, tattoos, her tight motorcycle clothes, and because she is so much older than I am.

But it's not only the passion, Dad. She's pregnant. Emily says that we will be very happy. She owns a trailer in the woods and has a stack of firewood for the whole winter. We share a dream of having many more children. Emily has opened my eyes to the fact that marijuana doesn't really hurt anyone. We'll be growing it for ourselves and trading it with the other people in our commune for all the cocaine and ecstasy we need.

In the meantime, we'll pray that science will find a cure for AIDS so that Emily can get better. She sure deserves it! Don't worry, Dad. I'm fifteen, and I know how to take care of myself. Someday, I'm sure we'll be back to visit so you can get to know your many grandchildren.

Love, your son, Ryan

p.s. Dad, none of the above is true. I'm over at Jason's house. I just wanted to remind you that there are worse things in life than my report card. Please call when it is safe for me to come home!

Random musician joke:
Saint Peter at the pearly gates:
To person one: "What did you do on Earth?"
"I was a surgeon. I helped the lame to walk."
"Well, go right on in through the pearly gates."
To person two: "What did you do on Earth?"
"I was a schoolteacher. I taught the blind to see."
"Fine. Go right on in through the pearly gates."

To person three: "What did you do on Earth?"
"I was a musician. I helped make sad people happy."
"You can load in through the kitchen."

A lawyer was working in his office late one night when Satan appeared.

"I can make it so you win every case in your career and make huge piles of money. In exchange, you will sell me your soul, your wife's soul, your children's souls, your parents' souls, your grandparents' souls, and the souls of all your friends."

The lawyer thought it over for a moment and then asked, "So, what's the catch?"

In Ireland, a drunk lad is traveling through the countryside and comes upon a priest in the middle of a river, giving baptisms. The priest calls out and asks the boy if he'd like to be baptized.

The boy says, "Sure, why not?"

So the drunk wades into the river and the priest dunks him in the water, and when he comes up sputtering, the priest says, "So, have ya found Jesus Christ yer lord and savior?"

The lad spits out some water and says, "No!"

The priest dunks him again. "Now have ya found Jesus Christ yer lord and savior?"

"No!"

The priest dunks him a third time. "Have ya found Jesus Christ yer lord and savior?"

The drunk lad yells, "No! Are ya sure this is where he went in?"

New tequila warning label:
Consuming tequila may make you think you are whispering when you're not; it may make you dance like a jerk; it may cause you to thay shings like zish; it may lead you to believe ex-girlfriends are dying to hear from you at 4:00 in the morning; it may make you forget about what just happened in your pants; it may lead you to believe you are invisible; it may make you believe people are laughing *with* you; it may make you believe you have mystical Kung Fu powers; it may make you roll over in the morning to greet an animal whose species you can't identify; and finally, it may cause a flux in the time-space continuum, where large gaps of time will literally disappear. Enjoy responsibly.

A Sunday school teacher told her students that she wanted each of them to have learned one fact about Jesus by the following Sunday. The following week, she asked each child in turn what he or she had learned.
Susie said, "He was born in a manger."
Bobby said, "He threw the money changers out of the temple."
Little Johnny said, "He has a red pickup truck, but he doesn't know how to drive it."
Curious, the teacher asked, "Now, where did you learn that, Johnny?"

"From my daddy," said Johnny. "Yesterday, we were driving down the highway and this red pickup truck pulled out in front of us, and Daddy yelled at him, 'Jesus Christ! Why don't you learn how to drive?'"

A policeman pulled over my buddy Rob for swerving in and out of lanes on the highway. He told Rob to blow into a breathalyzer.

"I can't do that, officer. I'm an asthmatic. I could get an asthma attack if I blow into that tube."

"Okay, we'll just get a urine sample down at the station."

"Can't do that either, officer. I'm a diabetic. I could get low blood sugar if I pee in a cup."

"All right, we could get a blood sample."

"Can't do that either, officer. I'm a hemophiliac. If I give blood, I could die."

"Fine, then, just walk this white line."

"Can't do that either, officer."

"Why not?"

"Because I'm *drunk*!"

My cousin Danny stood over his tee shot for what seemed an eternity, looking up, looking down, measuring the distance, figuring the wind direction and speed. Danny was driving his partner insane.

Finally, his exasperated partner said, "What's taking so long? Hit the damned ball!"

Danny answered, "My wife is up there, watching me from the clubhouse. I want to make this a perfect shot."

"Forget it, man," said his partner. "You don't stand a snowball's chance in hell of hitting her from here!"

―――――――

A fifteen-year-old boy came home with a Porsche. His parents began to yell and scream.

"Where did you get that car?"

He calmly told them, "I bought it today."

"With what money?" demanded his parents. "We know how much a Porsche costs!"

"Well," said the boy, "this one cost me fifteen dollars."

The parents began to yell even louder. "Who would sell a car like this for fifteen dollars?"

"It was the lady up the street," said the boy. "Don't know her name; they just moved in. She saw me ride past on my bike and asked me if I wanted to buy a Porsche for fifteen dollars."

"Oh, my goodness!" gasped the mother. "She must be a child abuser! Who knows what she will do next? John, you go right up there and see what's going on."

So, the boy's father walked up the street to the house where the lady lived and found her out in her yard, calmly planting flowers. He introduced himself as the father of the boy she had sold the Porsche to for fifteen dollars and demanded to know why.

"Well," she said, "this morning I got a phone call from my husband. I thought he was on a business trip, but I learned from a friend he has run off to Hawaii with his secretary and really doesn't intend to come back. He claimed he was really stranded and asked me to sell his new Porsche and send him the money. So I did."

Back when I was dating, I took this beautiful woman to the best restaurant in town. After that, we went to a killer concert, out for drinks, then back to her place for a little fun. Things were getting hot and heavy when suddenly, she stopped and said, "That's as far as we go for the first month."

I stood up, grabbed my jacket, and said, "Cool with me; see you next month."

After Mrs. Jacobs found out her husband was sterile, the couple decided to hire a proxy father to start their family. On the day the proxy father was to arrive, Mr. Jacobs kissed his wife and said, "I'm off to work, Lydia. The guy should be here soon."

Wouldn't you know it; a door-to-door baby photographer salesman came by half an hour later, hoping to make a sale. Mrs. Jacobs answered the door.

"Good morning, ma'am. You don't know me, but I've come to—"

"Oh, yes, I know why you're here. Harry told me you'd be coming soon."

"He did? But I—"

"Come right in! No use wasting time."

"Very well, then." The photographer took out his briefcase and sat down. "As you may already know, I've made a specialty of babies."

"Good, I'm glad," said Mrs. Jacobs. "That's just what Harry and I were looking for."

"I usually like to try two in the bathtub, one on the couch, and perhaps a couple on the bed," said the photographer. "The living room floor is fun too; you can really spread out."

"Bathtub? Living room floor? No wonder it never worked for Harry and me."

"Well, ma'am, none of us can guarantee a perfect one every time, but if we try several different positions and I shoot from six or seven different angles, I think you'll be quite pleased with the results."

"I certainly hope we can get this over with quickly." Mrs. Jacobs gasped nervously.

"Ma'am, in my line of work, a man must take his time. I'd like to be in and out in five minutes, but you'd be disappointed with that, I'm sure."

"Don't I know!" said Mrs. Jacobs.

The photographer pulled out a portfolio of his pictures.

"This one was done on top of a bus in downtown London," he said, showing Mrs. Jacobs the picture.

"Oh my God!" exclaimed Mrs. Jacobs, tugging on her handkerchief.

"And these twins turned out exceptionally well when you consider the fact that their mother was so difficult to work with."

He showed Mrs. Jacobs another picture.

"She was difficult?" questioned Mrs. Jacobs.

"Extremely," said the photographer. "I finally had to take her to Hyde Park to get the job done right. People were crowding around, four and five deep, just to get a good look."

"Four and five deep!" Mrs. Jacobs was amazed.

"Yes," said the photographer, "and for more than three hours, too. The mother was constantly squealing and yelling. I could hardly concentrate. Then it started getting dark, and I had to rush my shots. Finally, when the squirrels started nibbling on my equipment, I just packed it all in."

Mrs. Jacobs leaned forward. "You mean the squirrels actually chewed on your, um ... equipment?'

"Yes, ma'am. Thank God, no real damage was done. Well, we'll get to work as soon as I set up my tripod."

"Tripod?" Mrs. Jacobs looked extremely worried now.

"Of course. I need to use a tripod to rest my Canon on. It's much too big for me to hold while I'm getting ready for action. Uh ... ma'am?"

Have you ever gone to a gentlemen's club with a novice friend? Add copious amounts of alcohol, and your buddy sounds like this: "I think I love you. Here's my business card with my home phone, email, and address. Call me. You'll really love my wife!"

Great story for when he sobers up.

I lost my watch at a party once. I saw a drunk guy about to step on it while he was sexually harassing a young woman. I quickly walked over and punched him right in the nose and said, "Nobody does that to a woman, not on my watch!" (*Groan*)

A man tells his doctor that his wife hasn't wanted to have sex with him for the past seven months. The physician tells the man to bring his wife in so he can talk to her. When the wife comes to his office, the doctor asks her why she doesn't want to have sex with her husband anymore.

"For the last seven months," the wife replies, "every morning, I take a cab to work. I don't make much money, and my husband doesn't give me more than bus fare, so the cab driver always asks me, 'So are you going to pay today, or what?' I always give him an 'or what.' That makes me late to work. I'm late again, so the boss asks me, 'So are we going to dock your salary, or what?' That's another 'or what.' On the way home, I take the cab, and again, I don't have any money, so the cab driver asks me, 'So are you going to pay this time, or what?' And, again, I do an 'or what.' So, you see, doctor, when I get home, I'm all tired out, and I don't want any more sex."

The doctor thinks for a second. "So," he says, "are we going to tell your husband about this, or what?"

My mom has the most sensitive nose in the world. I truly believe she can smell my thoughts. My dad has the most sensitive gag reflex. I have both the super-sensitive nose and the crazy gag reflex. I won't go into the details, but you can imagine that these "attributes" have gotten me into trouble more than once with the women I have loved.

My old high school buddy Tom recently got married. Following the wedding, he laid down some rules.
"I'll be home when I want, if I want, and at what time I want," he insisted. "And I don't expect any hassle from you. Also, I expect a decent meal to be on the table every evening, unless I tell you otherwise. I'll go hunting, fishing, drinking, and golfing with my buddies whenever I want. Those are my rules. Any comments?"
His new bride replied, "No, that's fine with me. But just understand that there'll be sex here at seven o'clock every night—whether you're here or not."

My wife, Sally, hates the sight, smell, and taste of cucumbers, beets, and sushi. She doesn't want me to eat them. She doesn't want anyone within a five-mile radius of her to eat them. That makes me sneakier and stealthier than I've ever been about anything in my life.

A woman goes to the gynecologist for an exam. She puts her feet into the stirrups, and the doctor begins his exam. After a moment, the doctor remarks, "You have an unusually deep vagina."
The woman replies, "I know, but you don't have to say it twice."

My flight was too damned early. I hadn't had my coffee. I was surly, to say the least. The cheerful idiot at the counter was asking me the standard series of check-in questions.

"Sir, has anyone put anything in your baggage without your knowledge?"

I paused, trying to stay calm. "Ma'am, if anything was put in my baggage without my knowledge, *how the hell would I know*?" That's when my wife took over.

The first-grader walked up to the adult table at Thanksgiving and shouted, "Momma, give me a titty!"

We were all shocked. Turns out, my ex-sister-in-law breastfed her son until he was six years old.

She said, "Maybe y'all don't realize it, but this is really healthy for his immune system."

I said, "Six years? By this time, you ought to be able to safely dunk him in a barrel of polio."

A group of psychiatrists were attending a convention. Four of them decided to leave and walked out together. One said to the other three, "People are always coming to us with their guilt and fears, but we have no one that we can go to when we have problems."

The others agreed. Then one said, "Since we are all professionals, why don't we take some time right now to hear each other out?"

The other three agreed. The first then confessed, "I have an uncontrollable desire to kill my patients."

The second psychiatrist said, "I love expensive things, so I find ways to cheat my patients out of their money whenever I can so I can buy the things I want."
The third followed with, "I'm involved with selling drugs and often get my patients to sell them for me."
The fourth psychiatrist then confessed, "I know I'm supposed to, but no matter how hard I try, I can't keep a secret."

I grew up believing rabbits were deaf. Every Easter morning, I followed a trail of jelly beans from my bedroom to the dining room table. I couldn't wait to dig into my Easter basket. More jelly beans, multicolored marshmallow eggs, two Cadbury eggs, and one earless chocolate bunny. Thanks, Dad.

When I finished college, I went to work writing advertising music for a commercial music company on famed Music Row in Nashville. Sometimes clients had sales slogans they wanted me to incorporate into their ad music. A grocery store chain was particularly proud of their meat department. Their slogan? "You can beat our prices, but you can't beat our meat!" I'll just leave that right there.

You groggily pour that first cup of steamy hot, fog-cutting brain juice. You pull the cup to your lips, anticipating deliciousness. Suddenly, a sixty-pound flash of dog fur flies across the room and lands in your lap. An explosion of hot, molten lava showers down on you. What's the first word you scream? Mine rhymes with "brother mucker."

My uncle Tommy loved to dance, but he was also hard of hearing. We were having burgers in a local dive. He noticed a pretty girl leaning against the jukebox. She put on some Motown. Tommy said, "Oh yeah, gotta dance!"
He asked that girl if she wanted to take a spin around the dance floor.
She said, "Sorry, I'm concentrating on matrimony and would rather sit than dance."
He came back to our table. I asked him what happened.
"She said she was constipated on macaroni and would rather shit than dance."

A man walks home past a mental institution. One night, he hears the inmates chanting, "Three, three, three …"
He wonders what that's all about and ventures closer. The chant continues, "Three, three, three …"
He's at the gate now. He sees a peephole in the wall and decides he'll take a peek inside. Right when he looks, someone from the other side pokes a finger in his eye.
That's when he heard, "Four, four, four …"

So, last night, I was making the rounds in Nashville, pitching songs on Music Row with my wingman, Mick Jagger. It was great because we could get any meeting we wanted.

But then I had to rush to the airport to catch a flight back to reality.

A boy hears a banging noise and follows it into his parents' room, finding them in the midst of "schtupping." He's shocked. His father sees him and breaks out laughing. He tells his son that he'll meet the boy in his room in half an hour. In half an hour, he opens the door to the boy's room and finds the boy schtupping his grandmother. The father is shocked. The boy looks up and says, "See, it's not so funny when it's *your* mother!"

Last night, the police beat a Chinese man senseless. When questioned about the incident, the victim said the attack came out of nowhere.
"The cops asked me my name, and I answered them politely. All of a sudden, they Tased me and started slugging and kicking me. I don't know what set them off."
We asked the police department to comment on the incident, but so far, no response. A police brutality lawsuit is expected soon from Mr. Fuk Yu.

My Midwestern wife constantly feels the need to correct my "Southern" pronunciations. To her, these words have a silent *L: chalk, walk, caulk*. I disagree; they are *chock, wok, cock*. Today, my TV hero, Mike Rowe, laughingly corrected a woman's pronunciation when she stated on his show, "I used a lot of 'cock' on this." Chalk up one for me.

When I have a birthday, I thank all my friends for their birthday wishes. Then I thank those most responsible for my special day: my parents, the Catholic Church, and the "rhythm method." My dad always said he couldn't find his tambourine at 2:00 a.m.

A good-looking woman walks into a bar wearing a tube top. She raises her hand to signal the bartender for a beer, revealing that she does not shave under her armpits. Meanwhile, a sloppy drunk on the other side of the bar signals the bartender and says, "Buy that ballerina over there a drink on me."
The bartender replies, "What makes you think she's a ballerina?"
"Because," answers the drunk, "any chick that can lift her leg up that high has *got* to be a ballerina."

One beautiful sunshiny day when I lived in LA, I was walking down Ventura Boulevard, minding my own business, when a woman came up to me, pointed at my suede jacket, and screamed, "You know a cow was murdered for your jacket?"
I whispered to her in a psychotic tone, "I didn't know there were any witnesses. Now I'll have to kill you too."

We feed our dogs the very best food. So, it's not hunger that drives my goldendoodle to snatch and eat whatever catches her eye. Oh, look, she just pooped a rope—not poop that looks like a rope; an actual rope, three feet long!

Updating the collection of odd things she has ingested: eighty-seven pairs of cheap reading glasses; forty-three napkins; fourteen pairs of gloves; a wide assortment of socks and underwear; a tube of Neosporin; a jar of petroleum jelly; the handles off six steak knives; a two-pound block of cheddar cheese; a five-pound bag of gummy bears; at least a hundred ketchup, mustard, and taco sauce packets; and the latest, an entire bottle of the other dog's arthritis medicine! That one landed her in the emergency dog hospital to have her stomach pumped.

She's sweet and loving, but I can't leave the room for a second, because she's always looking for the next thing she can steal and eat! While I was writing this, she stole and ate an aluminum foil-wrapped rack of ribs off the kitchen counter. What's next?

While I was in LA, I used to watch Notre Dame football with my brother, John Duke, in Nashville and my son, Ryan Duke, in Chicago and text comments back and forth. Siri typed all my curses accurately, except the one that she typed *she-it*! You can take the boy out of the South, but you can't get the South out of his mouth, especially after a couple of beers.

A panda walks into a restaurant, sits down, and orders a sandwich. He eats the sandwich, pulls out a gun, and shoots the waiter dead. As the panda stands up to go, the manager shouts, "Hey! Where are you going? You just shot my waiter, and you didn't pay for your sandwich!"

The panda yells back at the manager, "Hey man, I'm a *panda*! Look it up!"

The manager Googles it and sees the following definition for *panda*: "A tree-dwelling marsupial of Asian origin, characterized by distinct black-and-white coloring. Eats shoots and leaves."

I am a big supporter of the Second Amendment, so I bought a musket. I've got the loading and firing sequence down to thirty seconds. I bite down on the paper cartridge and tear it open with my teeth. Push the striker (called a frissen) forward and pour a small amount of powder into the flash pan. Then I push the frissen back into position to cover the flash pan. Then I hold the musket with the muzzle pointing up and pour the rest of the powder into the barrel from the muzzle. Then I insert a lead ball into the barrel. Then I push the cartridge paper into the barrel (called the "wadding"). After that, I remove the ramrod from its storage pipe beneath the barrel and use it to push the wadding and the ball down the barrel. Then I quickly replace the ramrod in the storage pipe. Now I'm ready to raise the musket to a firing position, bracing the butt against my shoulder. Then I pull back the hammer, aim, and fire.

Now all I have to do is find a well-regulated state militia.

The agent for a beautiful young actress discovered one day that she had been selling her body for $1,000 a night. The agent freaked out because he had wanted to sleep with her for years and had no idea she could be obtained so easily. He approached her and said he loved her and wanted to make love to her. She agreed to an evening of sex but told him he would have to pay $1,000, just like the rest of her clients.

He said, "Hey now, don't I even get my 10 percent agent's fee deduction?"

She said, "No way; you pay, just like everybody else."

At midnight, the actress showed up at the agent's apartment, and they "bada-binged" to exhaustion. At 1:00 a.m., she felt a tap on her shoulder, and away they went again. At 2;00 a.m. came another tap on her shoulder. Now she was super impressed by her agent's longevity in the sack.

"My God," she whispered in the dark. "You are incredible in bed. I never knew how lucky I was to have you for an agent."

"I'm not your agent, honey," a strange voice answered. "He's at the door selling tickets."

Three guys walk into a bar. The bartender tells them, "If you can sit in my basement for a day, I'll give you free beer for the rest of your life."

The first guy tries it and walks out after five minutes, saying, "It's impossible; you got a swarm of nasty flies down there."

So the second guy tries his luck, but he can't stand it for more than an hour. Finally, the third guy goes down there.

When he returns a day later, the others ask him how he did it.

He says, "Easy! I dropped a deuce in one corner and sat in the other corner!"

We went out for a scotch tasting today. My wife, Sally, had some interesting ways of describing what she tasted. Here are her comments, in no particular order: turpentine and charcoal briquets. Burnt tires and cat urine. Fish heads and flu poop. And the one I liked the most, she said smelled like motor oil and formaldehyde, with a hint of frat-boy spew. She hates scotch.

I love scotch. Every time I begin to describe the taste, my speech pattern slows down, as if I'm tasting every word I say.

(Sip.) "Delicious. Buttered oats with honey, praline, dried fruit, and delicately spiced aromas that follow through on a super smooth, satiny entry to a dryish, medium-full body with buttercream, cocoa, toasted apples, and lush brown spice notes. Finishes with a long, sumptuous fade with accents of heather, peat moss, and sea air."

(Sip.) "Heaven."

Three nuns cleaning the convent on a hot day decide to remove their habits because of the intense heat—a sensible thing to do on such a sweltering day. The doorbell rings. They don't want anyone to see them naked.

One sister shouts out, "Who is it?"

"The blind man," a voice replies.

The three nuns decide to simply open the door because the man is blind.

He walks in, looks at the nuns, and says, "Nice tits! Where do you want me to install the blinds?"

Helayne was worried about Vince, so one day, she took him to the doctor. As the doctor called him in and looked him over, Vince began insisting, "There's nothing wrong with me. I know, because God takes care of me."

"What do you mean?" asked the doctor.

"Well," Vince responded, "at night, when I get up to go pee, he turns the light on and off for me."

The doctor decided he had better talk to both Vince and Helayne, so he called Helayne into the room and began to explain. "Vince says God turns the light on and off for him at night when he goes to the bathroom. Is it true that—"

"Dammit, Vince!" Helayne burst out. "How many times do I have to tell you not to piss in the refrigerator?"

A drunk man staggered to a seat on the subway next to a priest. The man's tie was stained, and his fly was open. He opened his newspaper and began reading. After a few minutes, the man turned to the priest and asked, "Say, Father, what causes arthritis?"

The priest replied, "My son, it's caused by loose living; being with cheap, wicked women; too much alcohol; contempt for your fellow man, sleeping around with prostitutes; and lack of a bath."

The drunk muttered in response, "Well, I'll be damned," and returned to his paper.

The priest, thinking about what he had said, nudged the man and apologized. "I'm very sorry. I didn't mean to come on so strong. How long have you had arthritis?"

The drunk answered, "I don't have it, Father. I was just reading here that the pope does."

I was frustrated. I needed to buy one damn bag of dog food. I'd been waiting in line at PetSmart for half an hour. All of a sudden, this jerk behind me piped up, "Looks like you've got a dog."

Dumbass, I thought to myself. Sarcastically, I said, "No, this is for me. I'm on the dog-food diet."

"Really?" replied the idiot.

"Yeah, I read that dog food is nutritionally balanced and the healthiest food in the world, so I've been eating nothing but dog food for the past month. My doctor is amazed; I've already lost fifty pounds eating this stuff."

The dummy predictably said, "Amazeballs!"

I continued, "Yeah, but I may have to quit because of the side effect."

Dum-dum asked, "Ugh, what side effect?"

"Yesterday, I almost got hit by a car crossing the street to sniff a bulldog's ass."

The mother superior at Saint Bernard's Convent School was chatting with some of the young students, and she asked them what they want to be when they grew up. A twelve-year-old jumped up and said, "I wanna be a prostitute!"

The mother superior fainted. When they revived her, she raised her head off the ground and groggily asked, "What … did … you … say?"

The young girl said, "I told you I want to be a prostitute."

"A prostitute!" Mother Superior said. "Oh, praise baby Jesus. I thought you said you wanted to be a Protestant!"

After a long chase, a highway patrol officer pulled a guy over, walked up to the driver's side window, and said, "Hey, buddy, don't you know what it means when you see my flashing lights behind you?"

"Yes sir, officer; I know."

"Then why the hell didn't you pull over immediately?"

Apologetically, he replied, "I would have, but last month, my wife ran off with a policeman, and I was afraid you were bringing her back!"

A man who thinks he's George Washington has been seeing a psychiatrist. He finishes up one session by telling him, "Tomorrow, we'll cross the Delaware and surprise them when they least expect it."

As soon as the patient leaves, the psychiatrist picks up the phone and says, "King George, this is Benedict Arnold. I have their plans."

Billy Bob was visiting New York City for the first time and staying at a swanky hotel. Before heading to his room, he asked the concierge what time meals were served.

"Breakfast is served from seven to eleven. Lunch is served from noon to three, and dinner is served from four to eight."

"Gosh almighty," replied Billy Bob. "That sure don't leave much time for sightseeing."

I grew up never really knowing if I deserved love. Eventually, I met someone who loved me, and I was finally able to accept myself. But once she got to know me well, she found me unbearable, so she left. The important point of this story is: stay hydrated.

When I was a young man pursuing my dreams, I had a huge fire in my belly to learn everything and do everything. Success was all that mattered. Now I know a lot, and I've done a lot. So, what happened to that young man chasing his dreams? The fire went out, but the belly remains.

I have several friends in showbiz who are both successful and rich. They are famous; I am not. I don't want their lives— too much responsibility. They have to shave and shower every day. Not me. I go to restaurants scruffy, in my shorts, flip flops, and tie-dyed T-shirts. Nobody knows me. Perfect. Another reason why I love my celebrity-adjacent life.

Everyone knows what a shart is. But did you know a sneeze/fart combo is called a snart? And when in a relationship is it okay to fart in front of each other? Squeakers don't count. From experience, I believe men will break wind first. Women take awhile. It took my wife fifteen years! She began with a few crop-dusting SBDs. I laughed. That opened the gates to a barrage of gurglers, schplatts, and turtlehead-gesnortches.

A cowboy appeared before Saint Peter at the pearly gates. "Have you ever done anything of particular merit?" Saint Peter asked.
"Well, I can think of one thing," the cowboy offered. "On a trip to the Black Hills out in South Dakota, I came upon a gang of bikers who were threatening a young woman. I directed them to leave her alone, but they wouldn't listen. So I approached the biggest, baddest, most tattooed biker and punched him in the face, kicked his bike over, ripped out his nose ring, and threw it on the ground. I yelled, 'Now, back off, or I'll kick the shit out of all of you!'"
Saint Peter was impressed. "Wow, when did this happen?"
"Couple of minutes ago."

On a beach vacation, the husband was catching some rays while his wife swam in the ocean. Suddenly, there was a riptide, and a woman was screaming as she struggled against it. The husband jumped up and said, "If someone can save my wife, I'll give you a hundred bucks!"

In a flash, the lifeguard sprang from his chair and into the water, saving the woman's life. When things had settled down, the lifeguard asked the husband, "Hey buddy, how 'bout that hundred bucks?"

The husband said, "When I made that offer, I thought my wife was drowning, but the woman you saved is actually my mother-in-law."

The lifeguard thought about it for a moment, then said, "Well, damn. I have the worst luck." Then he reached into his pocket and said, "All right, okay, how much do I owe you?"

A rather attractive woman goes up to the bar in a casual urban pub. She gestures alluringly to the barman, who comes over immediately. When he arrives, she seductively signals for him to bring his face close to hers. When he does so, she begins to gently caress his beard, which is full and bushy.

"Are you the manager?" she asks, softly stroking his face with both hands.

"Actually, no," he replies.

"Can you get him for me? I need to speak to him."

She runs her hands up, beyond his beard and into his hair.

"He's not here today," breathes the barman, clearly aroused. "Is there anything I can do?"

"Yes, there is. I need you to give him a message," she continues huskily, popping a couple of fingers into his mouth and allowing him to suck them gently. "Tell him that there is no toilet paper in the ladies' room."

There are only three words that make every red-blooded American drop to their knees and praise the Lord: *the Founding Fathers.* Did you genuflect? Yeah, me too. Think about this. They were in their early twenties. It was July in a sweltering-hot Philadelphia. They were dressed in multilayered suits. They wore powdered wigs under their sweaty hats, and there was no air-conditioning. Those conditions may have clouded their judgment. After all, they were slave owners creating documents about freedom. Now, since there's no record of them having superpowers enabling them to see into the future, maybe they didn't anticipate the military weaponry of the future and that assault rifles could fire hundreds of bullets in seconds. Maybe, just maybe, we need to tinker around with that Second Amendment, just a wee little bit.

I read that the United States is $23 trillion in debt and will never be able to pay back what was borrowed from countries like China. So please explain to me why some paper-pushing "public servant" is threatening to take my home over my kids' unpaid student loans?

Ain't love grand? It grows. It evolves. It dies. Here's an example I like to call, "excuses for not getting a vasectomy." In our thirties: "Sweetheart, what if, heaven forbid, you die, and after mourning the loss of the love of my life for an appropriate number of years, I remarry?"

In our forties: "Vasectomy? Honey, I'd really like to, but what if, during the surgery, an act of God occurs? A tornado or an earthquake hits and *boom*, the doctor slices away my precious little package, I could actually bleed to death on the operating table. Do you really want that on your conscience?"

In our fifties: "Vasectomy? Look, woman, we haven't had sex in years, and I don't see that changing anytime soon. Besides, you're too damn old to get pregnant. It's mine, and I'm keeping it. It's the only toy I have left from my childhood."

After delivering a powerful sermon on morality, Father Kelly asked all the virgins to please stand up. There was a little movement, but not one single woman stood up. Finally, a young girl with a newborn baby in her arms stood up.

Father Kelly said, "I'm afraid you misunderstood me. I asked that only virgins stand up."

The young girl replied, "I heard you just fine. You don't expect my three-month-old to stand up by herself, do you?"

We book it, a super-duper, all-inclusive vacay at a sweet Cancun resort. The plane takes off. The flight attendant brings us our Bloody Marys. *Wham, wham, wham, wham!* The kid kicking the back of my seat spills my Bloody on my new Tommy Bahama shirt. The parents do nothing. I could teach that kid's parents a thing or two about responsible parenting. My kids never misbehaved on flights. My kids slept on flights. My kids were drugged. That's when I came up with this perfect advertising slogan: "Benadryl, the 'flight time, kicking, crying, screaming, best sleep you ever got on an airplane' medicine."

I was late for my usual Sunday morning tee time. The course was crowded, and I couldn't find a place to park. I was frustrated driving up and down the parking lot and finding nothing, so I began to pray.

"Dear Lord, if you help me find a parking spot, I'll go to church every Sunday and quit drinking booze."

Just then, the perfect spot opened up, right next to the pro shop.

"Never mind. I found one!"

About the toilet—my wife doesn't believe me, but I really do aim. With laser-accurate, porcelain-denting power, I hit the target cleanly. Unfortunately, there is collateral damage as water is displaced from my mighty renderings. The taller a guy is, the greater the splatter. Look, we were meant to stand. The toilet seat could be raised to thigh height, or we could use a bigger target, a funnel, or a bucket. Until then, our wives can expect a continuation of the collateral splatter. Collateral Splatter, great band name.

My wife, Sally, is a gifted artist. Her paintings adorn the walls of our home. She can paint anything you can imagine in any style. The problem is, she's stuck. She wants to paint a series of works in an original style that's all her own, each unique in their own way and yet all identifiable as her personal little masterpieces. I need to think about this, so I head for the "boom-boom room." It's quiet in there. It's the think tank where I work out all my problems.

Aha! "Sally, I have it. Your series of original, uniquely identifiable works of art is ... now, hear me out. You take a photo, make a slide, project it up on your canvas, paint it realistically. Your new art should be ... poop. What? Honey, come back. No one's ever done it before! This is bigger than the pet rock! Honey?" (Door slams.)

This one really is a true story. There's a shop in London, England, called Richard III Camping Supplies. They have a Richard III mannequin and a sign in the window proclaiming, "This Is the Winter of Our Discount Tents." But what do they do in spring, summer, and fall? I don't know. Maybe it's time for them to get over the hump.

For many years, I was the advertising voice for Kentucky Fried Chicken. As part of that, I became KFC's voice for The Kentucky Derby. I love the Run for The Roses. I have a cousin who is from Kentucky. He has a hard time holding back the tears when 160,000 people at Churchill Downs sing "My Old Kentucky Home."

Seeking to console him, I told him that the song was never about mint-julep-drinking, well-to-do, white folks in bow ties and crazy hats celebrating the loss of their idyllic antebellum life in their beloved Kentucky. This Stephen Foster song was actually written about a slave whose Kentucky master had sold him to a slave master in the Deep South, where he would never know freedom and would surely be worked to death.

My cousin said, "Thanks, Pat, for screwing the one perfect memory I held of my childhood."

By the way, I also told my kindergarten class there's no Santa.

There are two kinds of drunks: happy drunks and angry drunks. I believe happy drunks far outnumber angry drunks. In a club, in a restaurant, at the ballpark, or on a plane, please keep serving the booze. It's a sedative. It's good medicine. The happy drunks will stay calm and friendly, harming no one. That one angry drunk can be restrained and removed. "One bad apple don't spoil the whole bunch, girl."

Jimmy's grandmother was sitting in a rocking chair on the front porch. Suddenly, her fairy godmother appeared and said she would grant the old woman three wishes.

Thinking it through, she said, "Well, I guess I would like to be rich." *Flash!* The rocking chair turned into solid gold. Grandma got excited. "Well then, it sure would be nice if I was young and beautiful."

Flash! She was now a young, gorgeous girl. Just then, a mangy old cat walked across the porch.

"For my last wish, do you think you could turn this old cat into a handsome prince?"

Flash! The cat was now the most gorgeous man she had ever seen. With a smile, this Adonis walked across the porch and hissed, "Now I bet you're sorry you had me fixed!"

Marital sleeping arrangements are complicated. I used to snore. Courtesy of my first wife, I have permanently bruised ribs to prove it. I got a CPAP machine. Best device ever, can't sleep without it. My current wife loves creative lighting. I like a pitch-black bedroom. I got a blackout mask. She snores. I got ear plugs. So, going to sleep for me means gearing up for complete sensory deprivation: CPAP, blackout mask, ear plugs, pillow over my head, and dog by my side. I sleep like a baby.

My son, Ryan, was zooming down I-65 at ninety miles an hour and got caught in a speed trap.

As the officer approached the car, he removed his mirrored sunglasses, smiled, and said, "Well, well, well, sonny boy, I've been waiting for you all morning."

Ryan quipped, "Well, officer, I got here as fast as I could."

Hashtag this, hashtag that, everything's a hashtag. Tweet this. No. I tried Twitter for a while. It was supposed to help my business. It didn't. I tried LinkedIn for years. It was supposed to help my business. It didn't. Instagram? Insta-who has time for that crap?

I'm on Facebook, for now. Even that's a bit shaky. Like it, love it, funny, sad, and angry buttons? I want a button that turns off all politics. Is that too much to ask? I guess it is, because that's how Facebook makes money. Facebook costs us nothing. It's free, but we pay for it with our time and personal data. I would gladly pay for it, if it had two additional buttons: "ads off" and "politics off." It never will. So I am trying my best to rein in my own political activities on social media. Besides, I've got way too much mindless TV to watch. Have you seen the latest episode of *Guilty Pleasures*?

The Thing. Gimme it. What thing? The Thing. Give it to me. I don't have it. Are you sitting on it? On what? *The Thing!* No. Look under the cushions. It's not there. I think you had it last. No, I didn't. Did you take it to the kitchen? No. Did you take it with you to the bathroom? No. Is it in your pocket? No. What's the dog chewing on? A bone. Well, maybe she ate it. Ate what? The Thing!

Goddamn. I said it. Was it offensive? Hell no. I'll say it again, and you'll be perfectly fine with it. Goddamn hurricanes. Goddamn child abuse. Goddamn cancer! It's all in how you use it. Consider it a prayer. God, will you please damn these atrocities? Thank you, God. Amen.

Concussions. I've had a bunch of them, from skateboarding as a kid, to junior-high football, to just being me as an adult. If I fall, I land on my extra-large *cabeza*. I recently Googled it. Head trauma kills the parts of your brain that feel and remember. That could be a good thing.

My ex was a tiny person, kinda like a child. When we got married, we headed south for our ultra-all-inclusive, platinum-level, sexy adult honeymoon at ... Disney World. Yes, I'm from Tennessee. No, I did not marry my eight-year-old cousin. And no, I did not enjoy "the happiest place on Earth." The only fun for me was witnessing Snow White cussing out one of the Seven Dwarfs for touching her inappropriately.

Recently, I went gator hunting in Louisiana with Troy Landry from the TV show *Swamp People*. My wife and I stayed at a hotel in the French Quarter in New Orleans. I got on a crowded elevator. Three party guys got on. We talked college football.

One of them said, "Dude, you sound like one of those TV or movie guy voices."

I said, "That's my job.

"No way! Oh my God! C'mon, man, narrate us!"

As I exited the elevator, I turned to them and said, "It was a night like any other—until three young men from the Midwest hit Bourbon Street. Then, all hell broke loose. Rated R, under seventeen not admitted."
They went nuts, high-fiving each other and screaming, "That guy's a badass!"
And the one who recognized my voice yelled, "I totally nailed that guy's voice!"
I could see them getting drunk and slurring that story to cute girls all over the French Quarter that night.

Like most guys, when I was young, the future was bright and all in front of me. I set goals. When I attained one goal, I aimed higher up the ladder of success. I moved up and up with each goal reached. What no one told me was that I would eventually reach a point in my career where there were no more goals to reach. I stopped. Looked around. And realized: the future was all behind me.

We moved from Los Angeles to Nashville a little over a year ago. We are still unpacking. We've emptied and put away the contents of over three hundred boxes. There are less than ten boxes remaining. This house has lots of storage: closets, drawers, a huge garage, and two walk-in attics. The way I see it, we will finally be through unpacking when we can't find a damn thing.

I don't believe in organized religion. If that works for you, I'm happy for you. What about God? I have more questions than answers. When it comes to him/her/it, I feel like I am in an obscure and complex version of poker in a pitch-dark room, with blank cards, for infinite stakes, with a dealer who won't tell me the rules and who smiles all the time.

When we were kids, my older brother was rough on me. *Merciless* is a better word for it. He was always trying to convince me that I was adopted. Dad, overhearing our discussion once, called me to the kitchen table and told me to have a seat.
With a serious tone, Dad said, "Pat, I hate to break this to you, but you were adopted."
I thought about that and said, "Fine, I want to meet my real parents. They've gotta be nicer than you!"
He said, "I don't think you understand; we are your real parents. Your adoptive parents will be here in fifteen minutes!"

This door-to-door salesman showed up on my front porch trying to sell me a fancy-schmancy home-security system. I told him, "My neighborhood is safe; I don't need it. I don't have time for this. My wife and I have dinner reservations. When we got home from dinner, his brochure was on my desk with a note that read, "Are you sure about that?"

I consider myself to be a master griller. I'm great with chicken and pork, but my specialty is steak. It's hard to describe the anticipation, the sense of euphoria I feel when a perfectly marbled T-bone or ribeye hits that hot grill with a loud sizzle. It must be the same feeling vegans get when they mow the lawn.

My buddy Richard never married. He spent forty years building a business empire, and in so doing, amassed quite a fortune. Last month, he invited me and a bunch of his old friends to his mansion for quite a surprise: his wedding. At the bachelor party, he showed us photos of his bride-to-be. We were shocked. His fiancée was drop-dead gorgeous and clearly thirty years his junior.
I had to ask. "How in the hell did you close that deal, Rich?"
He said, "I lied about my age. I told her I was ninety-six."

An eagle swoops down from the sky and eats a mouse. Three hours later, while the eagle is flying, the mouse sticks its head out of the eagle's butt and asks, "How high up are we?"
"About two thousand feet," the eagle replies.
The mouse replies, "Are you shittin' me?"

Let's play a game. It's called, "Tell Me Where I Am by What I'm Smelling." Okay, here we go. I smell Lysol and piss.

Anybody? Now I smell a whiff of onions, ass, and garlic. No? Next clue. Now I'm picking up the aroma of Jade East, sick-baby poop, crotch rot, and whiskey barf. Buzz in if you know. Still don't have it?

Okay, let's review before I give you the final clue. So far, we have: Lysol, piss, onions, ass, garlic, Jade East, sick-baby poop, crotch rot, and whiskey barf. Any idea? No? Ready for your final clue? Your final clue is ... curry.

(*Buzz.*) "Is it the back seat of a New York City cab?"

Ding ding ding ding ding ding ding! You win. You nailed it. And remember, folks, when you can't find your pecker, call a Checker! Checker Cab Company: We stink.

Addendum to previous joke:

When I lived in New York, I hated the cabs and the subway, but often, they were the only way. Cross-town buses were handy when it rained. I had a car service "guy" for airport trips. Stop. Car service instead of Uber or Lyft? Yes, because I prefer riding in the back of a Lincoln Town Car!

My best move was this: if I saw a limo driver leaning against his car, texting or reading the paper, waiting for his passengers, I struck up a conversation with him. I got right to the point.

"What's up? How long do you have to wait? An hour? Wanna make some quick money?"

"Hop in! Help yourself to the bar!"

"Don't mind if I do." I did this a lot. Limo ride and free booze—that's how I rolled in the Big Apple. (Also works in Chi-town.)

A cowgirl rides in the desert and comes upon a Native American lying naked with a hard-on.

She asks, "What are you doing?"

The naked man replies, "I'm finding out the time. It is 12:15."

The cowgirl looks at her watch and thinks, *Wow, it really is 12:15.* She continues on and sees another Native American lying naked with a hard-on.

She asks, "What are you doing?"

The naked man replies, "I'm seeing what time it is. It is 3:15."

The cowgirl looks at her watch, and that is the correct time. She continues and finds a third Native American lying naked on the ground, masturbating.

The cowgirl asks what he's doing, and he replies, "I'm winding my watch."

The best thing about politicians is ... hold on; I'm thinking. The best thing is that someday, their careers will end. Yay! So, let's borrow a real writer's words and be happy that we can vote their asses out. Know in your heart of hearts that someday soon, they will perish, perhaps in Shakespearean fashion. Out, out, shit candle! You were but a walking shadow, a poor player who struts and frets his hour upon the stage and then is heard no more. It was a tale performed by an idiot, full of sound and fury, signifying nothing.

Maryland, Virginia, West Virginia, Kentucky, Southern Indiana, Southern Illinois, Southern Missouri, Oklahoma, Texas, Louisiana, Mississippi, Alabama, Georgia, Florida, South Carolina, North Carolina, and Tennessee have a lot of wonderful things in common. This is the Holy Land, and not because it's the Bible Belt. Oh, no. It's holy because of the food.

Loosen your belt for whatever you want to call it, Southern cooking, soul food, or plain, old comfort food. If you can grow it, raise it, fish it, or herd it, Southern folks can "delicious-ize" it. A Southern "meat and three" can put you in a fully satiated, happy-tummy coma. And all that Gulf Coast seafood, yum to the yum. We have veggies too, like collard greens, fried okra, and beans—pinto, lima, green, black, red, every color—all seasoned with pork fat, ham hock, bacon drippings, healthy stuff.

Don't forget the buttermilk, barbecue, and cornbread. And be sure to finish off this holy miracle with a big ol' slice of pecan pie, key lime pie, banana pudding, or peach cobbler. This is heaven to me.

Unfortunately, this is hell for my "Yankee" wife. She can't stand Southern food. She's the only person I know who will venture into a world-famous barbecue joint and order a chicken Caesar salad, then wonder why her meal was so disappointing.

I always say, "Honey, that's like going to Benihana for a hot dog."

I have a great-great-uncle who fought in the Civil War. Sounds like I only had one, when in fact, every one of my many great-great-uncles and great-great-grandfathers fought in the Civil War. But this one in particular was shot in the hip with a lead mini-ball at The Battle of Stones River in Murfreesboro, Tennessee, a couple of miles from my house. Yeah, in two days of fighting, twenty-eight thousand young men died right over there.

Now, this particular uncle began seeing and conversing with dead people. Yep. So naturally, he became a preacher and started using his miraculous powers to convert sinners to Christianity. He was a huge success. He was a healer, an author, a visionary. People came from hundreds of miles away to hear him preach. Thousands of men, women, and children were "slain in the spirit" and dedicated their lives to Jesus because of my uncle. He could see relatives in heaven or hell and bring messages of warning or hope to their families.

Impressive, right? Perfect, until my cousin John and I realized his visions may have been hallucinations caused by lead poisoning from the mini-ball still lodged in his hip. If this happened today, he would have his own TV Show, *Mini-Ball Ministries*. And little old ladies would believe in his power to heal so much that they would gladly tithe their life's savings to him.

Did God grant him the power to heal? Who knows? All I know for sure is that tax-free racket is one hell of a profitable business model.

My voice has been on thousands of commercials and TV shows. Voice acting is a highly competitive field and takes a lot of hard work and dedication to reach a modicum of success. It looks easy. It's not. Still, a lot of people dream of making millions by simply talking. That's like shooting HORSE in the backyard with your friends and deciding you're ready for the NBA. The way I see it, voice acting is not a career; it's a severe mental illness and highly contagious.

In the voice-over business, I have fooled people about my meager talents to the point of being invited to voice-actor events where I received a bunch of pretty prestigious awards. My speech is always the same. I tell the audience that winning this award is the greatest event in my life, next to the birth of my first child—and I actually showed up for this!

Normally, I am cool, calm, and collected. Warning: do not exceed recommended dosages. But, but, but, melatonin? C'mon. It's an OTC. More is better, right? I need my sleepy. Gulp. (Time lapse.) One morning, my wife heard me through the door of my studio.

"I don't give a shit what the client can or can't afford. You're my agent, right? Well, do your f***ing job! Agent me. Get. Me. Paid. Asshole!" (*Tap, tap, tap.*) Sally whispered, "Honey, are you okay?"

"Hell yes, I'm okay! F*** that m-f-sob! He can *blank* my *blank*!"

Now, everyone needs their *blank blanked* from time to time, but folks, that rude, screaming, maniac is not me. That was Mr. Melatonin speaking. It can make you a wee bit aggressive.

But wait, there's more. I can also be undermedicated. Effexor was my drug of choice when I went through my nightmare divorce—twenty years ago. Now, I'm good to go. Screw Effexor. I said that a week ago when I went all macho: I can handle this cold-turkey, drug-detoxifying dookie—dizziness, confusion, loss of memory and balance, frustration, quick temper, angry outbursts, general weirdness.

I called my pool guy, salt of the Earth, really nice guy. No response. Left another message. "I need—no, I must have—repair work on the pool filter—*now!*"

Nada. Not a word from him. Squeaky wheel gets the worm, so I called again, all indignant, pissy, and righteously enraged. "I bought this piece of crap from you. It doesn't work. Now, get your ass over here and fix it—*now!*"

It was Sunday after 6:00 p.m. He called back in a quick minute, all apologetic.

"Sorry man; I haven't been taking calls, haven't even had my phone on. I've been going through a lot lately. My dad just died. We buried him this morning (*sniff*)."

I paused to consider his apology, personal pain, and loss. Then I said, "You call that an excuse?" (I didn't really say that, but I thought it loud enough for him to hear.) Who had taken over my body? Who would want to?

Don't worry. My mental state is fair and balanced now. Cool, calm, collected Pat has returned. (Sally: audible sigh of relief)

As a rule, I don't like anything with the word *fat* in it. Have you ever eaten a Fat Mo's burger? Not me. Against the rules. So, a few years back, when a Belgian-style ale became popular, I hit the brakes. It's called Fat Tire, so it's not for me, for obvious reasons. A few weeks ago, I hosted a party at my house, so I called my beer aficionado, connoisseur, and brewmeister, my son, Ryan, for recos. He knows beer. And an outdoor party in the summer in Tennessee needs an expert.

I loaded eight cases of the recommended beers into my coolers and covered them with 250 pounds of ice. The Modelo Especial, Tecate, and Corona Extra with limes went fast. The Yuengling and Sierra Nevada pulled a Houdini too. The next day, during the sultry sweat fest known as post-party cleanup, I reached down into the cooler's frigid ice water and pulled out a Fat Tire. I was hot; the beer was cold. Forget the rules. (*Pop, fizz, glugalugalug* ... ahhhhh.) I started singing.

"I'm in love with a beer I'm talkin' about. I'm in love with a beer I can't live without. I'm in love ..."

Okay, sorry, Grand Funk Railroad fans, but it's true. I am in love. And someday, I'm gonna marry that beer. It'll be a simple ceremony, mostly just me and FT and a couple hundred pounds of ice. What? She's FT to me. Never, ever, ever call your wife *fat*. I could call her Amber, because she is a beautiful, dark shade of amber. But I didn't want to draw unwanted attention to our relationship and have some prejudiced jerk freaking out about our mixed-race wedding.

———

Today, serendipitously, I co-wrote a joke with one of my comedy heroes, Randy Kagan. I met him in Chicago at Zanies Comedy Club when he was opening for Mitch Hedberg. (He thought I was the bouncer.) Now we are Facebook friends. Today, he got some pushback for quoting Obama on his page.

I threw him a lifeline and commented, "Politics is painful right now; tell us a joke."

He wrote, "Two Jews walk into a bar."

I wrote, "Their names are Jesus and Netanyahu."

He wrote, "The bartender said, 'We only serve Jews as an entrée!'"

He's a very twisted, funny guy. This is what he does for a living. My first ever collaboration with a comedy hero made my day. Y'all, check him out. Randy Kagan.

———

I've always had dogs. I love dogs, and they love me. Dogs have a sixth sense that with one whiff tells them I'm their guy, because they think my pockets are full of bacon. That's mainly because I wipe bacon grease on my jeans after breakfast. C'mon, napkins kill trees; trees provide oxygen— you do the math.

I have mostly had what are referred to as medium-sized dogs. My favorites are labs and doodles. They're gentle, loving, great with kids, intelligent, loyal, playful, sweet, easy to train, and big enough to cuddle. When I moved to a Manhattan high-rise apartment, management allowed dogs, but they couldn't weigh over twenty-five pounds. I've seen city rats bigger than that. Soon, I noticed that a lot of New York women carried their tiny pups in their purses wherever they went.

That's when the wisdom of tiny dogs hit me. Walking a dog late at night in New York City can be dangerous, but with a teacup-sized dog, all you have to do is hold them out the window of your high-rise apartment and squeeze.

An alligator walks into a bar, gives the bartender twenty bucks, and says, "Jack on the rocks."

The bartender pours the drink and, thinking the gator can't know much about money, gives him $2.50 in change and says, "I gotta tell ya, we don't get a lot of alligators in this bar."

The gator downs his Jack Daniels and says, "I'm not surprised, $17.50 a shot? I sure as hell won't be back!"

Today, being a parent is a lot like living with royalty.

Dad: "Sire, do the chicken nuggets meet your highness's royal expectations?"

Kid: "They are adequate. Now genuflect, kiss my ring, and back out of my room curtsying."

Everything we do is designed to please these diminutive masters of the universe. And if we displease them, they'll throw a royal tantrum or call the Department of Children's Services. They have that number on speed dial on their new iPhones. And they damn well better be given the latest game consoles and the newest games, or else.

And at school, there are no winners and no losers. Losing would permanently damage their sensitive psyches. Don't misunderstand me; they still play games, but they no longer keep score.

And now, writing in cursive is no longer being taught in grade school. What? I'm no Einstein, but I do have a question about that. If they can't write in cursive, what happens when these perfect little superbeings grow up and become the next generation of "instantly famous for nothing" social media stars? How in the hell are they going to be able to please their adoring fans without being able to sign autographs?

An old friend came to see me yesterday, somebody I haven't seen or heard from in over fifteen years. He said he missed me and that he was thinking about all the fun we used to have when we were both single and living in Chicago. We reminisced about the good old days. It occurred to me that he seemed to have forgotten that our friendship ended those many years ago on a bad note. I asked him if he remembered the last time we had seen each other. He didn't. He joked about having CRS disease—you know, Can't Remember Shit?

Then he got serious and told me he had early-onset dementia and was trying to reach out to old friends before everything he remembered disappears.

So I said, "I can help jog your memory, and then I've got a question for you. The last time I saw you, you were down on your luck, and you came to me asking for help. That was fifteen years ago, buddy, and since that day, I haven't seen you or the $10,000 I lent to you. Now, here's my question: will that be cash or check?"

The Athens of the South. Where is that? Nashville, Tennessee. Yeah, that was my hometown's original nickname. I know that's the truth because I've seen some really old collectible postcards. Anyway, Nashvillians loved the name so much, they built a full-sized replica of the Parthenon featuring a statue of Greek goddess Athena for the city's centennial celebration.

But does that name really reflect the spirit of the people? No. So they started calling Nashville "Music City, USA." Lots of music is made in Nashville. Truth be told, Nashville makes more Bibles than music, but "Bible City, USA" would be bad for the bar business, tourism, and strip clubs.

I don't know why, but wherever I go, complete strangers come up to me and are sure they know me. I worked in LA for many years doing voices on everything from movies to cartoons. A recent graduate of Columbia College Chicago wanted to "pick my brain," so we met in Studio City for drinks.

As we were talking, my friend Tom Kenny, aka SpongeBob Squarepants, joined us for a martini. I was facing the patio and a guy was waving at me, not in a weird way. So I nodded.

He jumped up from his table with a big grin and came to our table. He gave me a hug and asked how I've been. I introduced SpongeBob and the young girl I was meeting with; he shook hands with everyone and went back to his table. That guy who thought he knew me was Bryan Cranston.

My brother and I learned to play chess from our dad. I took a very important lesson away from all those hours of chess. Look at the king. He can only move one space at a time. He is weak and vulnerable. Your opponent wants to kill him. Now, look at the queen. She can move easily, anywhere she wants to go. She is the most powerful piece on the chessboard. Now, think about marriage.

Morris and his wife, Esther, went to the state fair every year, and every year, Morris would say, "Esther, I'd like to ride in that helicopter."

Esther always replied, "I know, Morris, but that helicopter ride is fifty dollars—and fifty dollars is fifty dollars."

One year, Esther and Morris went to the fair, and Morris said, "Esther, I'm eighty-five years old. If I don't ride that helicopter now, I might never get another chance."

Esther replied, "Morris, that helicopter is fifty dollars—and fifty dollars is fifty dollars."

The pilot overheard the couple and said, "Folks, I'll make you a deal. I'll take the both of you for a ride. If you can stay quiet for the entire ride and not say a word, I won't charge you! But if you say one word, it's fifty dollars."

Morris and Esther agreed, and up they went. The pilot did all kinds of fancy maneuvers, but not a word was heard. He did his daredevil tricks over and over again, but still not a word. When they landed, the pilot turned to Morris and said, "By golly, I did everything I could to get you to yell out, but you didn't. I'm impressed!"

Morris replied, "Well, to tell you the truth, I almost said something when Esther fell out, but you know—fifty dollars is fifty dollars."

Jimmy, a nudist buddy of mine, gets engaged to a beautiful woman named Wendy. He loves her so much he tattoos her name on his erect penis. When it's flaccid, the tattoo says WY. The couple decides to go to Jamaica on their honeymoon. Naturally, they choose a nudist resort. They have a wonderful time partying with their fellow nudists. Jimmy goes up to the bar to get a couple of rum drinks. He notices the bartender has WY tattooed on his penis. Amazed, he says, "I see your WY there, by any chance, is your wife's name Wendy?" The bartender says, "Oh no

Mon, I'm single. My tattoo says, "Welcome to Jamaica, have a wonderful day!"

A teacher was wrapping up class and started talking about the next day's final exam. He said there would be no excuses for not showing up, barring a dire medical condition or an immediate family member's death.

One smart-ass male student said, "What about extreme sexual exhaustion?" and the whole classroom burst into laughter.

After the laughter had subsided, the teach glared at the student and said, "Not an excuse; you can use your other hand to write."

Three guys go to a ski lodge, and there aren't enough rooms, so they have to share a bed. In the middle of the night, the guy on the right wakes up and says, "I had this wild, vivid dream of getting a hand job!"

The guy on the left wakes up, and, unbelievably, he's had the same dream, too.

Then the guy in the middle wakes up and says, "That's funny, I dreamed I was skiing!"

My girlfriend and I had been dating for over a year when we decided to get married. My parents helped us in every way, and my friends encouraged me. My girlfriend? She was a dream! There was only one thing bothering me: her younger sister. My prospective sister-in-law was twenty years of age and wore tight miniskirts and low-cut blouses. She would regularly bend down when near me, and I got many a pleasant view of her underwear. It had to be deliberate. She never did it when she was near anyone else. One day, little sister called and asked me to come over to check the wedding invitations. She was alone when I arrived. She whispered to me that soon I was to be married, and she had feelings and desires for me that she could not and did not really want to overcome. She told me that she wanted to make love to me just once before I got married and committed my life to her sister. I was in total shock and could not say a word.

She said, "I'm going upstairs to my bedroom, and if you want to go ahead with it, just come up and get me."

I was stunned. I was frozen in shock as I watched her go up the stairs. When she reached the top, she pulled down her panties and threw them down the stairs at me. I stood there for a moment, then turned and went straight to the front door. I opened the door and stepped out of the house and walked straight toward my car.

My future father-in-law was standing outside. With tears in his eyes, he hugged me and said, "We are very happy that you have passed our little test. We could not ask for a better man for our daughter. Welcome to the family!"

And the moral of this story is: always keep your condoms in your car.

A midget in Texas went to the doctor because his testicles ached almost all the time. The doctor told him to stand on the examining table and drop his pants. The doc put one finger under the midget's left testicle and told him to turn his head and cough—the usual method to check for a hernia. "Hmmm ..." mumbled the doc as he put his finger under the right testicle. He asked the midget to cough again. "Hmmm, I see the problem." The doctor reached for his surgical scissors.

Snip, snip, snip, snip, snip, snip, snip on the right side, then *snip, snip, snip, snip, snip, snip, snip* on the left side. The midget was so scared, he was afraid to look, but he noted with amazement that the snipping did not hurt. The doctor then told the midget to hop down off the table and pull his pants up and then to walk around and see if his testicles still ached.

The midget was absolutely delighted as he walked around the doc's office and discovered his testicles were no longer aching. He said, "That's perfect, doc, and I didn't even feel it! What did you do?"

The doctor replied, "I cut two inches off the top of your cowboy boots."

A woman is in bed with her lover, who also happens to be her husband's best friend. They make love for hours, and afterward, while they're just enjoying the afterglow, the phone rings. Since it is the woman's house, she picks up the receiver. Her lover looks over at her and listens, only hearing her side of the conversation.

She says in a cheery voice, "Hello? Oh, hi. I'm so glad that you called. Really? That's wonderful. I am so happy for you. That sounds terrific. Great! Thanks. Okay. Bye-bye."

She hangs up the telephone, and her lover asks, "Who was that?"

"Oh," she replies, "that was my husband telling me all about the wonderful time he's having on his fishing trip with you."

One weekend, the husband is in the bathroom shaving when the kid he hired to mow his lawn, a local kid named Bubba, comes in to pee. The husband slyly looks over and is shocked at how immensely endowed Bubba is. He can't help himself and asks Bubba what his secret is.

"Well," says Bubba, "every night before I climb into bed with a girl, I whack my penis on the bedpost three times. It works, and it sure impresses the girls!"

The husband was excited at this easy suggestion and decided to try it that very night. So before climbing into bed with his wife, he took out his penis and whacked it three times on the bedpost.

His wife, half-asleep, said, "Bubba? Is that you?"

To surprise her husband, an executive's wife stopped by his office. When she opened the door, she found him with his secretary sitting in his lap. Without hesitating, he dictated, "And in conclusion, gentlemen, budget cuts or no budget cuts, I cannot continue to operate this office with just one chair."

Joe enters the confessional and tells the priest that he has committed adultery.

"Oh, no," says the priest, thinking of the most promiscuous women in town. "Was it with Marie Brown?"

"I'd rather not say who it was."

"Was it with Betty Smith?"

"I'd rather not say," says Joe. The priest gives him absolution, and Joe leaves. While leaving the church, Joe's buddy asks if he received absolution.

"Yes, and two excellent leads!"

A successful businessman flew to Vegas for the weekend to gamble. He lost the shirt off his back and had nothing left but a quarter and the second half of his round-trip ticket. All he needed to do was somehow get to the airport, and then he'd be home-free. He went out to the front of the casino, where there was a cab waiting. He got in and explained his situation to the cabbie. He promised to send the driver money from home. He offered him his credit card numbers, his driver's license number, and his address.

The cabbie said, "If you don't have fifteen dollars, get the hell out of my cab!"

So, the businessman was forced to hitchhike to the airport and was barely in time to catch his flight.

One year later, the businessman, having worked long and hard to regain his financial success, returned to Vegas, and this time he won big. Feeling pretty good about himself, he went out to the front of the casino to get a cab ride back to the airport. Well, who should he see out there at the end of a long line of cabs but his old buddy who had refused to give him a ride when he was down on his luck.

The businessman thought for a moment about how he could make the guy pay for his lack of charity, and he hit on a plan. The businessman got in the first cab in the line. "How much for a ride to the airport?" he asked.

"Fifteen bucks," came the reply.

"And how much for you to give me a blow job on the way?"

"What? Get the hell out of my cab."

The businessman got into the back of each cab in the long line and asked the same questions, with the same result. When he got to his old friend at the back of the line, he got in and asked, "How much for a ride to the airport?"

The cabbie replied, "Fifteen bucks."

The businessman said, "Okay," and off they went. As they drove slowly past the long line of cabs, the businessman gave a big smile and thumbs-up sign to each of the other drivers.

During a funeral, the pallbearers accidentally bump into a wall and hear a faint moan. They open the casket and find out that the woman is actually alive. She lives for ten more years and then dies. There is another funeral for her. At the end of the service, the pallbearers carry out the casket. As they are walking out, the husband cries out, "Watch out for that wall!"

My only other blonde joke:
A blonde walks into a drugstore and asks the pharmacist for some bottom deodorant. The pharmacist, a little bemused, explains to the woman that they don't sell anything called bottom deodorant and never have. Unfazed, the blonde assures him that she has been buying the stuff from this store on a regular basis and would like some more.
"I'm sorry," says the pharmacist. "We don't have any."
"But I always get it here," says the blonde.
"Do you have the container it comes in?"
"Yes!" says the blonde. "I will go and get it."
She returns with the container and hands it to the pharmacist, who looks at it and says to her, "This is just a normal stick of underarm deodorant."
The annoyed blonde snatches the container back and reads out loud from the container: "To apply, push up bottom."

Satan appeared before a small-town congregation. Everyone started screaming and running for the front church door, trampling each other in a frantic effort to get away. Soon, everyone was gone except for an elderly gentleman, who sat calmly.
Satan walked up to him and said, "Don't you know who I am?"
The old man replied, "Yep, sure do."

Satan asked, "Aren't you going to run?"

"Nope, sure ain't," said the old man.

Satan asked, "Why aren't you afraid of me?"

The old man replied, "Been married to your sister for over forty-eight years."

One day, Bill complained to his friend that his elbow really hurt. His friend suggested that he go to a computer at the drugstore that can diagnose anything quicker and cheaper than a doctor could.

"Simply put in a sample of your urine, and the computer will diagnose your problem and tell you what you can do about it. It only costs ten dollars."

Bill figured he had nothing to lose, so he filled a jar with a urine sample and went to the drugstore. He found the computer, poured in the sample, and deposited the ten dollars. The computer started making some noise, and various lights started flashing. After a brief pause, out popped a small slip of paper, on which was printed: "You have tennis elbow. Soak your arm in warm water. Avoid heavy lifting. It will be better in two weeks."

Later that evening, while thinking how amazing this new technology was and how it would change medical science forever, he began to wonder if this machine could be fooled. He mixed together some tap water, a stool sample from his dog, and urine samples from his wife and daughter. To top it off, he masturbated into the concoction. He went back to the drugstore, located the machine, poured in the sample, and deposited the ten dollars.

The computer again made the usual noise and printed out the following message: "Your tap water is too hard. Get a water softener. Your dog has worms. Get him a prescription at your vet. Your daughter is using cocaine. Put her in a rehabilitation clinic. Your wife is pregnant with twin girls. They aren't yours. Get a lawyer. And if you don't stop jerking off, your tennis elbow will never get better."

A man and his wife are at a restaurant, and the wife keeps staring at an old drunk guy slugging down martinis at a nearby table.
Her husband asks, "Do you know him?"
"I'm afraid so," sighs the wife. "He's my ex. He took to drinking right after we divorced seven years ago, and I hear he hasn't been sober since."
"My God!" says the husband. "Who would think a person could go on celebrating that long?"

An investigative journalist went to Afghanistan to study the culture and was shocked to discover that women were made to walk ten paces behind the men. She asked her guide why, and he said, "Because they are considered of lesser status."
Outraged, the journalist went home. A year later, she returned to cover violence in the region and was surprised to see the women walking ten paces ahead. Excited by

what she was witnessing, she turned to her guide and this time asked, "What has changed?"

The guide answered, "Land mines."

In a murder trial, the defense attorney was cross-examining the coroner.

"Before you signed the death certificate, did you take the pulse, listen to the heart, or check for breathing?"

"No."

"So, when you signed the death certificate, you weren't sure the man was actually dead, were you?"

"Well, the man's brain was in a jar on my desk, but I suppose he could have still been practicing law for a living."

A real woman is a man's best friend. She will inspire him to accomplish great things, to live without fear and forget regret. She will enable him to express his deepest feelings and give in to his most intimate desires. She will make him feel as though he is the most handsome man in the world and enable him to feel confident, strong, sexy, seductive, and invincible. No, wait ... sorry ... I'm thinking about bourbon.

A family was driving behind a garbage truck. Suddenly, a dildo came flying out of the truck and smacked into the windshield.

Embarrassed, and to spare her young son's innocence, the mother turned around and said, "Don't worry, dear. That was just an insect."

"Wow," the boy replied. "I'm surprised it could get off the ground with a dick that big!"

A recently widowed lady was sitting on a beach towel at Cocoa Beach, Florida. She looked up and noticed that a man her age had walked up, placed his blanket on the sand nearby, and begun reading a book. Smiling, she attempted to strike up a conversation with him.

"Hello, sir; how are you?"

"Fine, thank you," he responded and turned back to his book.

"I love the beach. Do you come here often?" she asked.

"First time since my wife passed away last year," he replied and again turned back to his book.

"Do you live around here?" she asked.

"Yes, I live over in Suntree," he answered and then resumed reading.

Trying to find a topic of common interest, Sarah persisted. "Do you like pussycats?"

With that, the man threw his book down, jumped off his blanket onto hers, tore off both their swimsuits, and gave her the most passionate ride of her life!

As the cloud of sand began to settle, Sarah gasped and asked the man, "How did you know that was what I wanted?"

The man replied, "How did you know my name was Katz?"

At two in the morning, I got pulled over by a cop. The policeman inquired, "Where are you going at two a.m.?"
I quickly replied, "Officer, I'm headed to a lecture about the damage drinking, late nights, and lack of sleep do to the body."
Curious, the cop asked, "Who will be giving this lecture?"
"My wife, sir."

Two families move from Pakistan to America. When they arrive, the two fathers make a bet to see, in a years' time, which family will have become more Americanized. A year later, they meet again.
The first man says, "My Americanization is going very well. I'm driving a Ford F-150, my son is playing Little League baseball, I had breakfast at McDonald's, and I'm on my way to pick up a case of Budweiser. How are you doing?"
The second man replies, "Great. Now go back to your shithole country, towel head!"

A Jewish man living in Moscow applies to move to Israel. At 3:00 a.m., there's banging on his door. It's the KGB.
"You! Jew! You applied to move to Israel?" He nods.
"Here in Russia, don't you have food to eat?"
"Yeah, I can't complain."
"And here in Russia, don't you have place to live?"
"Yeah, yeah, I can't complain."
"And here in Russia, don't you have job to work at?"
"Yeah, I can't complain."

"So, Jew, why did you apply to move to Israel?"
"Because there, I *can* complain."

A reporter is conducting an interview in Saudi Arabia:
Reporter: "Name?"
Man: "Abdul."
Reporter: "Sex?"
Man: "Four or five times a week."
Reporter: "No, I mean, like male or female!"
Man: "Yes, yes, females everywhere, sometimes camel."
Reporter: "Holy cow!"
Man: "Yes, cow, sheep, animals in general—just not pig."
Reporter: "But isn't that hostile?"
Man: "Yes, horse-style, doggy-style, many style."
Reporter: "Oh, dear."
Man: "No, not deer. Too hard to catch."

A man is getting into the shower just as his wife is finishing up her shower, when the doorbell rings. The wife quickly wraps herself in a towel and runs downstairs. When she opens the door, there stands Bob, the next-door neighbor. Before she says a word, Bob says, "I'll give you eight hundred bucks to drop that towel."
After thinking for a moment, the woman drops her towel and stands naked in front of Bob, and after a few seconds, Bob hands her $800 and leaves. The woman wraps back up in the towel and goes back upstairs. When she gets to the bathroom, her husband asks, "Who was that?"

"It was Bob, the next-door neighbor," she replies.

"Great," the husband says, "did he say anything about the eight hundred bucks he owes me?"

A doctor, a lawyer, and a biker were having a lively conversation at a bar. After a sip of his martini, the doctor said, "You know, tomorrow is my anniversary. I got my wife a diamond ring and a new Mercedes. I figure that if she doesn't like the diamond ring, she will at least like the Mercedes, and she will know that I love her."

After finishing his scotch, the lawyer replied, "Well, on my last anniversary, I got my wife a string of pearls and a trip to the Bahamas. I figured if she didn't like the pearls, she would at least like the trip, and she would know that I love her."

The biker then took a big swig from his beer and said, "Yeah, well, for my anniversary, I got my old lady a T-shirt and a vibrator. I figured if she didn't like the T-shirt, she could go fuck herself."

An American soldier serving in World War II had just returned from several weeks of intense action on the German front lines. He had finally been granted R&R and was on a train bound for London. The train was very crowded, so the soldier walked the length of the train, looking for an empty seat. The only unoccupied seat was directly adjacent to a well-dressed middle-aged lady and was being used by her little dog.

The war-weary soldier asked, "Please, ma'am, may I sit in that seat?"

The English woman looked down her nose at the soldier, sniffed, and said, "You Americans. You are such a rude class of people. Can't you see my little Fifi is using that seat?"

The soldier walked away, determined to find a place to rest, but after another trip down to the end of the train, he found himself again facing the woman with the dog. Again, he asked, "Please, lady. May I sit there? I'm very tired."

The English woman wrinkled her nose and snorted. "You Americans! Not only are you rude; you are also arrogant." The soldier didn't say anything else; he leaned over, picked up the little dog, tossed it out the window of the train, and sat down in the empty seat. The woman shrieked and railed and demanded that someone defend her and chastise the soldier.

An English gentleman sitting across the aisle spoke up. "You know, sir, you Americans do seem to have a penchant for doing the wrong thing. You eat holding the fork in the wrong hand. You drive your automobiles on the wrong side of the road. And now, sir, you've thrown the wrong bitch out the window."

Another train joke? Why not?

A Russian, a Cuban, an American, and a lawyer are riding together on a train. The Russian takes a bottle of the best vodka out of his pack, pours some into a glass, drinks it, and says, "In Russia, we have the best vodka in the world;

nowhere in the world you can find vodka as good as one we produce in Ukraine. And we have so much of it, we can just throw away." As he says this, he opens the window and throws the rest of the bottle through it. All the others are quite impressed.

The Cuban takes a pack of Havanas, unwraps one, lights it, and begins to smoke, saying, "In Cuba, we have the best cigars of the world: Havanas. No country in the world produces such a fine cigar, and we have so many of them that we can just throw them away." He opens the window and throws the pack of Havanas through it. Once again, everybody is quite impressed.

At this point, the American stands up silently, opens the window, and throws the lawyer through it.

An elderly husband whispers in his wife's ear at the bar, "Do you remember the first time we had sex together over fifty years ago? We went behind the bar, where you leaned against the back fence and I made love to you."

"Yes," she says, "I remember it oh so well!"

"Okay," he says, "let's go there again, and we can do it for old times' sake."

"Oh, Marvin, you old devil, that sounds like a crazy but good idea!"

A police officer sitting in the next booth hears their conversation and, having a chuckle to himself, he thinks, *I've got to see these two old-timers having sex against a fence. I'll just keep an eye on them so there's no trouble.* So he follows them. The elderly couple walks haltingly along, leaning on each other for support and aided by walking sticks. Finally, they get to the back of the tavern and make their way to the fence The old lady lifts her skirt, and the old man drops his trousers. As she leans against the fence, the old man moves in. Then, suddenly, they erupt into the most furious sex the policeman has ever seen. This goes on for about ten minutes while both are making loud noises and moaning and screaming. Finally, they both collapse, panting, on the ground. The policeman is amazed. He thinks he has learned something about life and old age that he didn't know.

After about half an hour of lying on the ground recovering, the old couple struggles to their feet and puts their clothes back on. The policeman is still watching and thinks, *This is truly amazing. I've got to ask them what their secret is.*

As the couple passes, he says to them, "Excuse me, but that was something else. You must've had a fantastic sex life together. Is there some sort of secret to this?"

Shaking, the old man is barely able to reply. "Fifty years ago, that wasn't an electric fence."

Final thought

Be open. Whether it's fate, karma, luck, or God, opportunities are sent our way every day. Be open. Believe in the innate goodness of everyone in your life. Be helpful. Be kind. Be open. If you are struggling, don't close down. Bring the light, the hope, and the love. You will be rewarded. Goodness, kindness, and happiness are coming your way right now. Be open.

That's all I've got—for now.
Keep your wife happy.
Don't forget to flush.

Talking to myself: "Hold it. What about old folks and retirement jokes?"
"Didn't we cover that?"
"Not enough for my liking, you old fart!"
"Okay, okay, *okay*! You want more? Consider this your encore."

A five-year-old boy went to visit his grandmother one day. While playing with his toys in her bedroom while she was dusting, he looked up and said, "Grandma, how come you don't have a boyfriend?"
Grandma replied, "Honey, my TV is my boyfriend. I can sit in my bedroom and watch it all day long. The TV evangelists keep me company and make me feel so good. The comedies make me laugh. I'm really happy with the TV as my boyfriend."
Grandma turned on the TV, and the reception was terrible. She started adjusting the knobs, trying to get the picture in focus. Frustrated, she started hitting the backside of the TV, hoping to fix the problem. The little boy heard the doorbell ring, so he hurried to open the door, and there stood Grandma's minister.
The minister said, "Hello, son, is your grandma home?"

The little boy replied, "Yeah, but she's in the bedroom bangin' her boyfriend."

A little old lady is sitting on a park bench in Miami Beach. A man walks over and sits down on the other end of the bench. After a few moments, the woman asks, "Are you a stranger here?"
He replies, "I used to live here years ago."
"So, where were you all these years?"
"In prison," he says.
"For what did they put you in prison?"
He looks at her and very quietly says, "I killed my wife."
"Oh," says the woman. "So, you're single."

Four old men were out golfing.
"These hills are getting steeper as the years go by," one complained.
"These fairways seem to be getting longer too," said one of the others.
"The sand traps seem to be bigger than I remember them too," said the third senior.
After hearing enough from his buddies, the oldest and the wisest of the four of them, at eighty-seven years old, piped up and said, "Just be thankful we're still on the right side of the grass!"

Three old, retired guys are out walking. First one says, "Windy, isn't it?"
Second one says, "No, it's Thursday!"
Third one says, "So am I. Let's go get a beer."

A man was telling his neighbor, "I just bought a new hearing aid. It cost me $6,000, but it's state of the art. It's perfect."
"Really," answered the neighbor. "What kind is it?"
"Twelve thirty-five."

Morris, an eighty-two-year-old man, went to the doctor to get a physical. A few days later, the doctor saw Morris walking down the street with a gorgeous young woman on his arm. A couple of days later, the doctor spoke to Morris and said, "You're really doing great, aren't you?"
Morris replied, "Just doing what you said, doc: 'Get a hot mama, and be cheerful.'"
The doctor said, "I didn't say that. I said, 'You've got a heart murmur. Be careful.'"

Two little old ladies had been very long-time close friends. But being old-fashioned, each went to a retirement home of her own respective religion. It was not long before Mrs. Murphy felt very lonesome for Mrs. Cohen, so one day, she asked to be driven to the Jewish home to visit her old friend. When she arrived, she was greeted with open arms, hugs, and kisses.

Mrs. Murphy said, "Don't be holdin' back, Mrs. Cohen. How do you like it here?"

Mrs. Cohen went on and on about the wonderful food, the facility, and the caretakers Then, with a twinkle in her eye, she said, "But the best thing is that I now have a boyfriend."

Mrs. Murphy said, "Now isn't that wonderful! Tell me all about it."

Mrs. Cohen said, "After lunch, we go up to my room and sit on the edge of the bed. I let him touch me on the top, and then on the bottom, and then we sing Jewish songs."

Mrs. Murphy said, "For sure, 'tis a blessing. I'm so glad for you, Mrs. Cohen."

Mrs. Cohen said, "And how is it with you, Mrs. Murphy?"

Mrs. Murphy said it was also wonderful at her new facility and that she also had a boyfriend.

Mrs. Cohen said, "Good for you! So what do you do?"

"We also go up to my room after lunch and sit on the edge of the bed. I let him touch me on top, and then I let him touch me down below."

Mrs. Cohen said, "Yes? And then?"

Mrs. Murphy said, "Well, since we don't know any Jewish songs, we screw."

A Florida couple, both well into their eighties, went to a sex therapist's office. The doctor asked, "What can I do for you?"

The man said, "Will you watch us have sexual intercourse?"

The doctor raised his eyebrows, but he was so amazed that this elderly couple would be asking for sexual advice, he agreed. When the couple finished, the doctor said, "There's absolutely nothing wrong with the way you have intercourse."

He thanked them for coming, wished them good luck, charged them fifty dollars, and sent them on their way. The next week, the couple returned and asked the sex therapist to watch again. The sex therapist was a bit puzzled but agreed. This happened several weeks in a row. The couple made an appointment, had intercourse with no problems, paid the doctor, and then left.

Finally, after six weeks of this routine, the doctor said, "I'm really puzzled, and I must ask, just what are you trying to learn from these sessions?"

The old man replied, "We're not trying to learn anything. Edna's married, so we can't go to her house. I'm married, so we can't go to my house. The Holiday Inn charges $125. The Hilton charges $150. If we have sex here, it costs me fifty bucks, and I get $43 back from Medicare."

An elderly Irishman had been drinking at a pub all night. The bartender finally said that the bar was closing. So, the old Irishman stood up to leave and fell flat on his face. He tried to stand one more time—same result. He figured he'd crawl outside and get some fresh air, and maybe that would sober him up. Once outside, he stood up and fell flat on his face. So, he decided to crawl the four blocks to his home. When he arrived at the door, he stood up and again fell flat on his face. He crawled through the door and into his bedroom. When he reached his bed, he tried one more time to stand up. This time, he managed to pull himself upright, but he quickly fell right into bed and was sound asleep as soon as his head hit the pillow.

He was awakened the next morning by his wife standing over him, shouting, "So, you've been out drinking again!"

"What makes you say that?" he asked, putting on an innocent look.

"The pub called—you left your wheelchair there again."

A little old lady answered a knock on the door one day, only to be confronted by a well-dressed young man carrying a vacuum cleaner.

"Good morning," said the young man. "If I could take a couple of minutes of your time, I would like to demonstrate the very latest in high-powered vacuum cleaners."

"Go away!" said the old lady. "I haven't got any money! I'm broke!" And she proceeded to close the door.

Quick as a flash, the young man wedged his foot in the door and pushed it wide open. "Don't be too hasty!" he said. "Not until you have at least seen my demonstration." And with that, he emptied a bucket of horse manure onto her hallway carpet.

"If this vacuum cleaner does not remove all traces of this horse manure from your carpet, madam, I will personally eat the remainder."

The old lady stepped back and said, "Well I hope you've got a good appetite, because they cut off my electricity this morning!"

Two ninety-year-old men, Moe and Sam, have been friends all their lives. It seems that Sam is dying of cancer, and Moe comes to visit him every day.

"Sam," says Moe, "you know how we have both loved baseball all our lives, and how we played minor-league ball together for so many years? Sam, you have to do me one favor. When you get to heaven—and I know you will go to heaven—somehow, you've got to let me know if there's baseball in heaven."

Sam looks up at Moe from his deathbed and says, "Moe, you've been my best friend for many years. This favor, if it is at all possible, I'll do for you."

And shortly after that, Sam passes on.

It is midnight a couple of nights later. Moe is sound asleep when he is awakened by a blinding flash of white light, and a voice calls out to him, "Moe ... Moe ..."

"Who is it?" says Moe, sitting up suddenly. "Who is it?"

"Moe, it's me, Sam."

"Come on. You're not Sam. Sam just died."

"I'm telling you," insists the voice, "it's me, Sam!"

"Sam? Is that you? Where are you?"

"I'm in heaven," says Sam, "and I've got to tell you, I've got really good news and a little bad news."

"So, tell me the good news first," says Moe.

"The good news," says Sam, "is that there is baseball in heaven. Better yet, all our old buddies who've gone before us are there. Even better, we're all young men again. And even better than that, it's always springtime, and it never rains or snows. And best of all, we can play baseball all we want, and we never get tired!"

"Really?" says Moe. "That is fantastic, wonderful beyond my wildest dreams! But what's the bad news?"

"You're pitching next Tuesday."

A family brings their elderly mother to a nursing home. While sitting in her new room, she slowly starts to lean over sideways in her chair. Two attentive nurses immediately straighten her up. After a while, she starts to tilt to the other side. The nurses rush back to put her upright. This goes on all morning.

Later, the family arrives and asks, "Are they treating you all right, Mom?"

She replies, "It's fine, I guess, except for one thing."

"What is it, Mom?"

"They won't let me fart."

Last joke coming up.

The parish priest went on a fishing trip. On the last day of his trip, he hooked a monster fish and proceeded to reel it in. The guide, holding a net, yelled, "Look at the size of that son of a bitch!

"Son, I'm a priest. Your language is uncalled for!"

"No, Father, that's what kind of fish it is—a son-of-a-bitch fish!"

"Really? Well, then, help me land this son of a bitch!"

Once it was in the boat, they marveled at the size of the monster.

"Father, that's the biggest son of a bitch I've ever seen."

"Yes, it is a big son of a bitch. What should I do with it?"

"Why, eat it, of course. You've never tasted anything as good as a son of a bitch!"

Elated, the priest headed home to the rectory. While unloading his gear and his prize catch, Sister Mary inquired about this trip.

"Take a look at this big son of a bitch I caught!"

Sister Mary gasped and clutched her rosary. "Father!"

"It's okay, Sister. That's what kind of fish it is—a son-of-a-bitch fish!"

"Oh, well then, what are you going to do with that big son of a bitch?"

"Why, eat it, of course. The guide said nothing compares to the taste of a son of a bitch."

Sister Mary informed the priest that the new bishop was scheduled to visit in a few days and that they should fix the son of a bitch for his dinner.

"I'll even clean the son of a bitch," she said. As she was cleaning the huge fish, the friar walked in.

"What are you doing, Sister?"

"Father wants me to clean this big son of a bitch for the new bishop's dinner."

"Sister! I'll clean it if you're so upset! Please watch your language!"

"No, no, no, it's called a son-of-a-bitch fish."

"Really? Well, in that case, I'll fix up a great meal to go with it, and that son of a bitch can be the main course! Let me know when you've finished cleaning that son of a bitch."
On the night of the new bishop's visit, everything was perfect. The friar had prepared an excellent meal. The wine was fine, and the fish was excellent. The new bishop said, "This is great fish; where did you get it?"
"I caught that son of a bitch!" proclaimed the proud priest. The bishop's eyes opened wide, but he said nothing.
"And I cleaned the son of a bitch!" exclaimed the sister. The bishop sat silent in disbelief.
The friar added, "And I prepared the son of a bitch, using a special recipe!"
The new bishop looked around at each of them. Slowly, a big smile crept across his face as he said, "You fuckers are my kind of people!"

Yes, I'm ending the book on an F-bomb. It's the only one in the entire book. (Actually, there are three.) Gimme a break. I need a nap now. I'm finished, old, exhausted—but still laughing. Where's my bong?

THE END

Oh, crap, one more joke, and I swear it is the last one. This one is for my son, Ryan. No one tells it better.

Back in the days when England and Spain ruled the seas, they were always on the lookout for Captain Redshirt and his band of merciless pirates. No one was braver than Captain Redshirt, and his crew were savage, bloodthirsty killers.

One evening, a British ship issued a challenge. The captain screamed, "First mate, fetch me my red shirt!"

He donned the shirt, and the pirate crew fought mightily and won. A couple days later, five British ships challenged Captain Redshirt. He again commanded his first mate to fetch his red shirt; he did, and once again, the pirate crew fought heroically and won. The first mate was curious about the red shirt.

The captain said, "The red shirt is for the crew. If I get seriously injured, they won't see the blood from my wounds, and they'll continue to fight on."

The next day, an entire Spanish Armada appeared on the horizon. Captain Redshirt looked at his crew, looked at the Spanish ships, thought for a moment, then screamed, "First mate, fetch me my brown pants!"

About the Jokester

Who the hell is Pat Duke? I'll answer your question with a question. Do you now, or have you ever, watched TV? Well, I'm a guy whose voice you have heard your entire life.

Yep. Those commercials you hate? Me. Not all of them, but over ten thousand of them. From beer to burgers to chicken to pizza to cars to cereal to airlines to tires to cookies to trucks to ketchup to shampoo and everything in between, you have heard my voice for over thirty years on your TV.

For the past several years, I have been narrating TV shows—lots of them, including over thirteen years on the runaway smash-hit TV show *Swamp People* on The History Channel, which is watched by millions of fans each week in every English-speaking country in the world.

Phew! That's a hell of a career, right? Yes, and not quite. I have worn several other hats in the entertainment business, mostly in music. In order, they have been: drummer; singer; Emmy-award-winning composer; arranger; producer; publisher; artist promoter for a major record label; and movie producer.

All that to say, I've lived my entire life around some of the funniest people on the planet.

To Hear Pat Duke:
https://youtube.com/user/dukevoice1
www.patduke.com

To Book Pat Duke:
Dean Panaro Talent
10999 Riverside Dr., Suite 301
Los Angeles, CA 91602
818-660-0633
dean@deanpanarotalent.com

Stewart Talent Chicago
400 North Michigan Avenue
Chicago, IL 60611
312-943-3131
sheila@stewarttalent.com

Innovative Artists New York
235 Park Avenue South, 10th floor
New York, NY 10003
212-253-6900
allan.duncan@iany.com

Cover Art by Kenneth Benner
https://kenbennerillustration.weebly.com/